3-D Cross Stitch

3-D Cross Stitch

More than 25 Original Designs

Meg Evershed

Sterling Publishing Co., Inc.
New York

For Mike, Elizabeth and Annie, with thanks for all the cleaning, cooking, ironing, etc.

3-D Cross Stitch

Meg Evershed

Published by Sterling Publishing Company, Inc.
387 Park Avenue South, New York, N.Y. 10016

First published in the United Kingdom by Hamlyn,
an imprint of Octopus Publishing Group Limited

Distributed in Canada by Sterling Publishing c/o Canadian Manda Group,
One Atlantic Avenue, Suite 105 Toronto, Ontario, Canada M6K 3E7

© Octopus Publishing Group Limited 1999

Library of Congress Cataloging–in–Publication Data Available
10 9 8 7 6 5 4 3 2 1

Executive Editor MIKE EVANS
Senior Editor NINA SHARMAN
Editor ROSEMARY WILKINSON
Art Director KEITH MARTIN
Designer LISA TAI
Production JOANNA WALKER
Special Photography by Jon Bouchier
Illustrations by JANE HUGHES

Printed in Hong Kong
All rights reserved
ISBN: 0-8069-5895-2

Contents

Foreword

Cross stitching is a relaxing hobby enjoyed by many people. Wide ranges of fabrics, threads and accessories allow stitchers to produce wonderful examples of their skills to enhance their own homes, or to give as gifts. A cross-stitched sampler can mark a special event – a birth or an anniversary, for example – and pictures of all types bring great pleasure when presented to family and friends.

3-D Cross Stitch aims to help you take your skills a step further and make imaginative and attractive items that will do more than hang on the wall. Some pieces have a practical use and some, like the cross stitched village, are purely decorative, but each piece may be picked up and viewed from all sides.

You can use your own memories and imagination to create a three-dimensional piece if you wish. It's not essential to copy the colour scheme and stitching instructions exactly, as it is when working a picture. When you stitch a model cottage, for example, you may have stayed in such a place while on holiday, and you can change details such as the colour of the curtains, or the position of the climbing roses to make the cottage more like the one you rented last summer. You won't spoil the design, and you will be making something to remind you of a special time.

Similarly, change the stitching if you wish. Do you hate working French knots – lots of stitchers do! Don't let anything spoil your enjoyment, but make the flowers from cross stitches if you prefer, or use appropriately coloured seed beads. Making changes like this will not affect the overall success of the piece you are stitching. The aim is to enjoy every moment of making it, and produce something that gives you pleasure and a sense of achievement.

The designs provide suitable projects for anyone wanting to try something new. Do read through all the instructions before you begin stitching, and then you will be set to enjoy a new dimension in cross stitch!

Clockwise from top left: The Parish Church tower; Cockleshell House; Silhouette Trinket Box and the Doll's House Sofa

SCENTED TOWN HOUSES

Each of these four colourful scented houses is stitched and assembled in the same way, so choose your favourite colour, or make all four – they present a very attractive sight when standing together in a row. These pieces have a fairly simple shape, and would be an ideal project if you have not tried three-dimensional work before.

Lavender House

This miniature scented house is both decorative and useful. Hang it among your clothes or stand it in your home so that everyone can enjoy the sweet scent.

walls

roof

DMC	Anchor		DMC	Anchor		Back stitch	
						DMC	Anchor
413	236		746	386		796	134
341	117		318	399		413	236
796	134		743	305		986	246
793	176		818	271		961	76
905	257		961	76		793	176
986	246		415	398			

Measurements

The finished size of the scented houses is 9cm tall, 4.3cm wide and 4cm deep (3½ x 1¾ x 1⅝in).

Materials

- *For the walls*: Piece of white 22 count hardanger measuring 20 x 13cm (8 x 5⅛in).
- *For the roof*: Piece of sky blue 28-count Jobelan evenweave measuring 10 x 15cm (4 x 5⅞in)
- *For the base*: Royal blue or white felt measuring 7 x 6cm (2¾ x 2 ⅜in)
- 75cm (¾yd) royal blue ribbon, 3mm (⅛ in) wide
- DMC or Anchor stranded embroidery cotton in the colours shown on the charts
- 1 piece 7-mesh plastic canvas measuring 16 x 14cm (6⅜ x 5½in)
- A small quantity of dried lavender or pot pourri
- Tapestry needle size 26 or 28
- Sewing needle
- Matching sewing thread
- Embroidery frame if required

To work the embroidery

Prepare the hardanger fabric as explained in the techniques section, see page 109. Mark the outline of the walls and the centre of the design with basting stitches. Make sure there is a margin of at least 2cm (¾in) around the walls on all sides, as this will be needed when you come to stitch the house together. The irregular shape will not have an obvious centre, but begin stitching in the middle of the fabric.

Work the Lavender House using one strand of embroidery thread, and each cross stitch is worked over one square of the hardanger fabric. Follow the chart given for the walls, and work all the cross stitches before you begin the back stitching, which is used to define certain areas of cross stitch, and to add tiny details. Work all the back stitch in the colours indicated on the charts. Some back stitches are worked over two or more squares, so follow the chart carefully.

Working the roof

Mark the roof area to be stitched on the blue Jobelan, making sure you leave a margin all around it. Follow the chart for the roof on page 10 and work in back stitch using one strand of DMC 796/Anchor 134 over two threads of the fabric.

Wash and dry the pieces as described in the techniques section on page 110.

Assembling the house

Assemble Lavender House by the lacing method, following the instructions on pages 12–13.

The Lacing Method of Construction

Two methods of constructing three-dimensional pieces are described: the lacing method given here, and the sandwich method described on page 26. The lacing method is faster and holds the fabric to the plastic canvas more firmly, but the sandwich method is easier and better for small pieces, or those with an irregular shape. Most of the pieces can be constructed using either method, but the lacing method is most suitable for the scented houses as there is only one layer of fabric for the perfume to pass through.

Lacing embroidery to plastic canvas

1 To make the flat embroidery into a little house it must be mounted on plastic canvas walls. From the plastic, using the templates given opposite, cut out two gable walls, two side walls, two half roof pieces and a base.

half of roof
cut 2

base
cut 1

side wall
cut 2

gable wall
cut 2

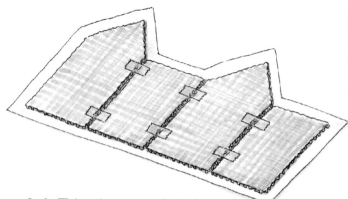

2 △ Take the cross stitched walls, and trim the fabric around the embroidered shape, leaving a margin of 2cm (¾in) outside the outline of basting stitches. Do not cut between the walls; they should be in one long strip. Lay the fabric face down on a flat working surface, and place the plastic canvas walls on top, matching them to the embroidered shape. Stick the plastic canvas pieces to each other with sticky tape, but leave a tiny gap between the walls so that they can bend round to form the house.

3 Fold the excess fabric onto the plastic canvas, snipping carefully into the corners to make it lie flat. At the top of the gables, fold one side of the fabric over the other to prevent the plastic point pushing through the fabric.

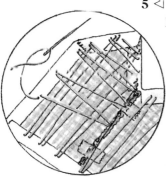

4 △ Using a long length of matching sewing thread, lace the fabric over the plastic pieces by passing the needle from the top to the bottom, taking small stitches in the fabric margins. Keep the thread taut, but not too tight or you will distort the shape of the walls.

5 ◁ Fold in the corners and hold them in position with small stitches. If the fabric does not seem to be secure, lace it horizontally across the end pieces, slipping the needle through the holes in the plastic canvas and returning to take a small stitch in the fabric at the side. This will hold the cross-stitched design to the plastic canvas frame of the house as securely as possible.

6 The roof and base are mounted on the plastic using the same lacing method. Hold the plastic roof pieces together with sticky tape, leaving a slight gap between them so that they will bend to form the ridge. Lay the embroidered roof face down on the work surface and place the plastic canvas roof pieces on top, making sure the ridge is in the middle of the fabric. Lace the roof fabric over the plastic canvas. Mount the plastic canvas base piece on the felt in the same way.

Assembling the house

1 ▷ Take the walls, and bend them around at right angles to each other, so that they form the shape of a house. The edge of the side wall should meet the edge of the gable wall. Using matching sewing thread, ladder stitch these two edges together, as described in the section on stitches, see page 112. Take care to match the brickwork pattern as closely as possible.

2 ◁ Fold the sides of the roof into an inverted V-shape, with the ridge in the centre. Place it in position on top of the walls with the ridge at the top point of the gables. Make sure the overhang is equal on both sides. Ladder stitch the roof to the walls, taking a small stitch in the roof fabric, followed by a small stitch in the top edge of the walls. Begin stitching at a corner, work up one side of the gable to the ridge, down the other side and then along the side wall.

3 If you find it difficult to manoeuvre your needle round the corners, a pair of tweezers will be helpful. You may also leave some of the stitches loose when negotiating a corner, and gently pull on the thread to bring the pieces together.

4 Put the lavender or pot pourri inside the house. Push the base into the bottom of the house where it should fit just inside the walls. Ladder stitch it into position, making sure that the house will not wobble when it stands upright.

5 Fold the ribbon in half and tuck in the ends, securing them with a few small stitches. Sew the ribbon neatly to the middle of the roof ridge.

Cockleshell House

Cockleshell House is the same size and shape as Lavender House, but has a different pattern.
The shell motif above the windows and doors gives this design a distinctive appearance.

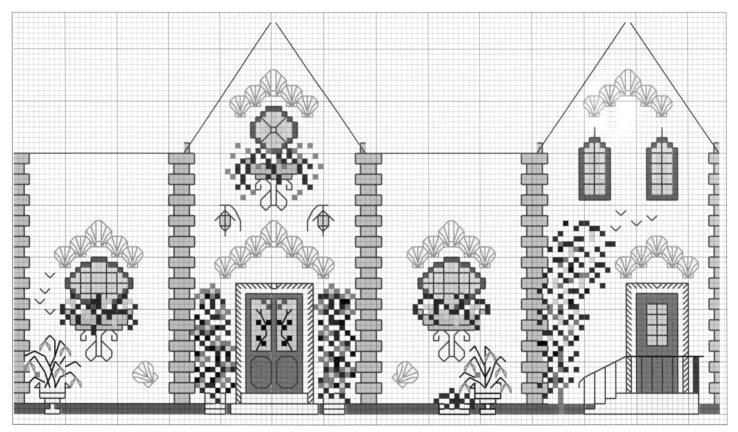

walls

DMC	Anchor		DMC	Anchor		Back stitch	
3731	77		318	399		DMC	Anchor
3326	36		319	683		3731	77
818	271		904	258		319	683
3747	117		317	400		317	400
746	386		743	305		799	145
415	398		799	145		318	399

Measurements

The finished size of the scented houses is 9cm tall, 4.3cm wide and 4cm deep (3½ x 1¾ x 1⅝in).

Materials

The sizes and quantities of the materials are the same for all the scented houses, but different colours are required for each design.

- *For the walls*: Piece of white 22-count hardanger measuring 20 x 13cm (8 x 5⅛ in)
- *For the roof*: Piece of pink 28-count Jobelan evenweave measuring 10 x 15cm (4 x 5⅞in)
- *For the base*: Pink or white felt measuring 7 x 6cm (2¾ x 2⅜in)
- 75cm (¾yd) pink ribbon, 3mm (⅛in) wide
- DMC or Anchor stranded embroidery cotton in the colours shown on the chart
- 1 piece 7-mesh plastic canvas measuring 16 x 14cm (6⅜ x 5½in)
- A small quantity of dried lavender or pot pourri
- Tapestry needle size 26 or 28
- Sewing needle
- Matching sewing thread
- Embroidery frame if required

To work the embroidery

Follow the instructions given for the Lavender House to prepare the fabric (see page 11), making sure there will be a margin of at least 2cm (¾in)

around the design on all sides. Follow the chart for the walls of the Cockleshell House opposite. Work the cross stitch using one strand of thread at a time over one square of the fabric. Work all the back stitch in the colours indicated on the chart, over one or two squares as shown.

Working the roof

The Cockleshell House roof is worked in the same way as the Lavender House roof. Prepare the pink Jobelan fabric and follow the same chart, but work the design using DMC 3731/Anchor 77.

Wash and dry the pieces as described in the techniques section on page 110.

Assembling the house

Assemble Cockleshell House by the lacing method following the instructions on pages 12–13.

Wisteria House

One of the most attractive sights in early summer is a house draped in wisteria. The delicate colour and graceful flowers make any house look like a desirable residence.

walls

DMC	Anchor		DMC	Anchor		Back stitch	
3042	870		700	229		DMC	Anchor
211	342		369	1043		552	99
210	108		3731	77		645	273
209	109		818	271		700	229
552	99		645	273			
702	226		3072	234			

Measurements

The finished size of the scented houses is 9cm tall, 4.3cm wide and 4cm deep (3½ x 1¼ x 1⅝in).

Materials

The sizes and quantities of the materials are the same for all the scented houses, but different colours are required for each design.

- *For the walls*: Piece of white 22-count hardanger measuring 20 x 13cm (8 x 5⅛in)
- *For the roof*: Piece of violet coloured 28-count Jobelan evenweave measuring 10 x 15cm (4 x 5⅞in)
- *For the base*: Purple or white felt measuring 7 x 6cm (2¾ x 2⅜in)
- 75cm (¾yd) purple ribbon, 3mm (⅛in) wide
- DMC or Anchor stranded embroidery cotton in the colours shown on the chart
- 1 piece 7-mesh plastic canvas measuring 16 x 14cm (6⅜ x 5½in)
- A small quantity of dried lavender or pot pourri
- Tapestry needle size 26 or 28
- Sewing needle
- Matching sewing thread
- Embroidery frame if required

To work the embroidery

Follow the instructions given for the Lavender House to prepare the fabric (see page 11), making sure there will be a margin of at least 2cm (¾in) around the design on all sides. Follow the chart for the walls of Wisteria House opposite. The cross stitch is worked using one strand of thread at a time over one square of the fabric. Work all the back stitch in the colours indicated on the chart. Some back stitches are worked over two or more squares, so follow the chart carefully.

Working the roof

The roof of Wisteria House is worked in the same way as the Lavender House roof. Prepare the violet Jobelan fabric and follow the same chart, but work the design using DMC 552/Anchor 99.

Wash and dry the pieces as described in the techniques section on page 110.

Assembling the house

Assemble Wisteria House by the lacing method, following the instructions given on pages 12–13.

St Clement's House

This house derives its name from the orange and lemon trees standing around the walls. It would be most appropriate to fill it with some citrus-scented pot pourri.

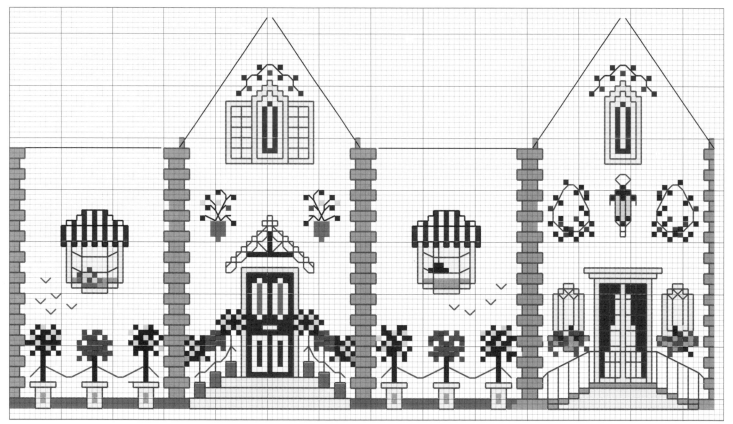

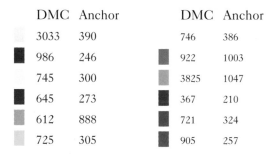

walls

DMC	Anchor		DMC	Anchor
3033	390		746	386
986	246		922	1003
745	300		3825	1047
645	273		367	210
612	888		721	324
725	305		905	257

Back stitch

DMC	Anchor
922	1003
645	273
986	246

Measurements
The finished size of the scented houses is 9cm tall, 4.3cm wide and 4cm deep (3½ x 1¾ x 1⅝in).

Materials
The sizes and quantities of the materials are the same for all the scented houses, but different colours are required for each design.

To work the embroidery

Follow the instructions given for the Lavender House to prepare the fabric (see page 11), making sure there will be a margin of at least 2cm (¾in) around the design on all sides. Follow the chart for the walls of St Clement's House opposite. Work the cross stitch using one strand of thread at a time over one square of the fabric. Work all the back stitch in the colours indicated on the charts, over one or two squares as shown.

Working the roof

St Clement's House roof is worked in the same way as the roof of Lavender House. Prepare the apricot Jobelan fabric, and follow the same chart, but work the design using DMC 922/Anchor 1003.

Wash and dry the pieces as described in the techniques section on page 110.

Assembling the house

Assemble St Clement's House by the lacing method, as described on pages 12–13.

- *For the walls*: Piece of white 22-count hardanger measuring 20 x 13cm (8 x 5⅛ in)
- *For the roof*: Piece of apricot coloured 28-count Jobelan evenweave measuring 10 x 15cm (4 x 5⅞in)
- *For the base*: Apricot or white felt measuring 7 x 6cm (2¾ x 2 ⅜in)
- 75cm (¾yd) apricot ribbon, 3mm (⅛in) wide
- DMC or Anchor stranded embroidery cotton in the colours shown on the chart
- 1 piece 7-mesh plastic canvas measuring 16 x 14cm (6⅜ x 5½in)
- A small quantity of pot pourri
- Tapestry needle size 26 or 28
- Sewing needle
- Matching sewing thread
- Embroidery frame if required

CROSS STITCH VILLAGE

English villages can be the most picturesque places. Here are cross-stitched models of some of the buildings that may be found in the English countryside. Stitch the whole village if you want to impress, or make an individual piece as a special gift.

The Flint Cottage

Cottages built of flint can be seen in many parts of England, especially in East Anglia.
The Wellington boots and rabbit hutch outside the back door suggest that this is a family home.

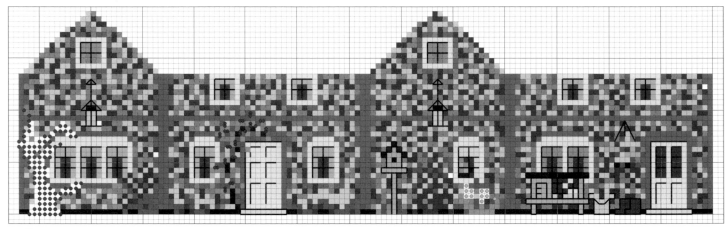

walls

DMC	Anchor
904	258
762	234
535	400
310	black
3776	1001
blanc	white
989	261
644	830
972	298
890	1044
647	1040
500	879
349	13
729	890
809	130
646	1040

ridge of roof

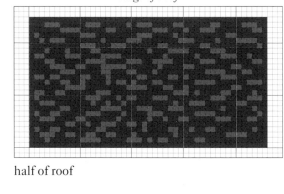

half of roof

Back stitch

DMC	Anchor
310	black

French knots

DMC	Anchor
blanc	white
972	298
890+989	1044+261
349	13
809	130

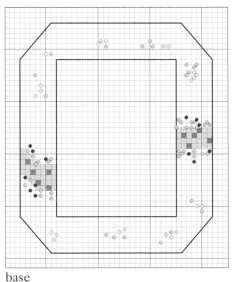

base

Measurements

The finished size of the Flint Cottage is 6cm tall, 8.2cm wide and 7cm deep (2⅜ x 3 ¼ x 2¾in).

Materials

In this design, none of the Aida fabric shows through – the whole area is covered with cross stitches. Preferably use a fairly dark colour, but any neutral shade will give a good result.

- *For the walls*: Piece of antique sage 18-count Aida measuring 23 x 10cm (9⅛ x 4in)
- *For the roof*: Piece of antique sage 18-count Aida measuring 10.5 x 11cm (4¼ x 4⅜in)

N.B. You will need a piece of interfacing the same size as the embroidery fabric for each piece of stitching you mount using the sandwich method, see pages 26 to 27.

- *For the base*: Piece of green 28-count Jobelan evenweave measuring 12.5 x 11cm (5 x 4⅜in)
- Piece of felt in a neutral colour, such as fawn or dark green, measuring 8.5 x 7.5cm (3⅜ x 3in)
- DMC or Anchor stranded embroidery cotton in the colours shown on the chart
- 1 piece of 7-mesh plastic canvas measuring 17 x 12cm (6¾ x 4¾in)
- Tapestry needle size 26 or 28
- Sewing needle
- Matching sewing thread
- Embroidery frame if required

To work the embroidery

Prepare the fabric as described in the techniques section on page 109, marking the outline of the cottage walls on the larger piece of Aida fabric with basting stitches. Make sure you leave a margin of at least 2 cm (¾ in) around the shape of the walls on all sides, as this will be needed when you come to mount the fabric on the plastic. Mark the centre of the design, but with this irregular shape it will be difficult to be accurate, so begin stitching where you judge the centre approximately to be.

Follow the chart for the walls on page 22, using one strand of thread at a time. Don't worry if you make mistakes in the flint pattern. The aim is to give an overall effect of flint walls and small errors will make no difference to the general appearance. Work each of the cross stitches shown on the chart over one square of the fabric, and complete all the cross stitches before you begin to work the French knots and back stitch.

• All the back stitch for the flint cottage is worked using DMC 310/Anchor black.

• The red French knots on the front wall represent berries on the climbing shrub. Keep them small by using only one strand of thread, and winding it twice around the needle.

• The creeper around the window on the side wall is worked using one strand of DMC 890/Anchor 1044, and one strand of DMC 989/Anchor 261 together in the needle. Wind the thread around twice to give a crunchy effect.

Working the roof

Stitch the roof on the smaller piece of Aida fabric. The two sides of the roof are identical, so the chart for the roof shows only one side. Mark the centre, and stitch the central ridge line first, making sure your stitching will be positioned with a margin of at least 2 cm (¾ in) around it on all sides. Stitch the roof pattern below the centre ridge, then turn the work around and stitch the same pattern on the other side of the ridge.

Working the base

Follow the chart to work the base on the green Jobelan evenweave. Work the cross stitches first, working each stitch over two threads of fabric, then the French knots. You do not need to be strictly accurate with the French knots – just dot them around in small groups to represent flowers.

When you have worked all the pieces for the Flint Cottage, wash and dry them as described in the techniques section.

Assembling the cottage

Most of the pieces in this book may be mounted using the lacing method described on page 12, but another technique, the sandwich method, is described on page 26 and you may prefer to mount the Flint Cottage in this manner.

1 Whichever method you choose, mount the walls, roof and base on the plastic canvas as a first step in assembling the cottage.

2 This cottage is assembled in the same way as the town houses (see page 13) and as shown on page 27. Bend the walls around and stitch the side seam, then stitch the roof to the walls.

3 ◁ The cottage now has to be attached to the base. Stand it in the middle of the base, so that the paths are close to the doors, and ladder stitch the two pieces together. Pass the needle up through the base and take a small stitch in the bottom edge of the walls, then push the needle back down through the holes in the plastic canvas, and bring it up again through the next hole.

Work all around the walls of the cottage, joining it securely to the base.

4 Finally, sew or stick felt to the underside of the base, covering all the internal stitching.

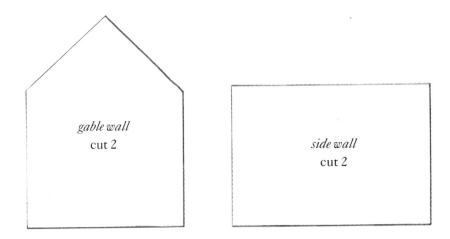

gable wall
cut 2

side wall
cut 2

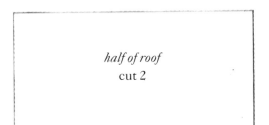

half of roof
cut 2

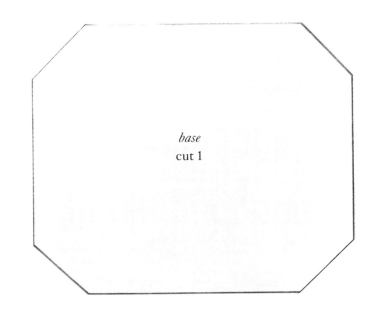

base
cut 1

The Sandwich Method of Construction

Here is an alternative method for mounting your cross stitch on the plastic canvas – the sandwich method. You may find it easier but it takes a little longer to achieve. Some pieces, such as the money boxes (see pages 58–64), will need to be made using this method, and small and irregularly shaped pieces will be easier to mount in this way. Otherwise the choice is yours.

Sandwiching the plastic canvas

1 ▷ Every piece of embroidery to be mounted using the sandwich method needs a piece of interfacing the same size. Use a light or medium weight sew-in interfacing. Lay the interfacing on the working surface, and place the embroidery on top of it, right side uppermost. Sew the two pieces together using back stitch and work close to the cross stitches, about 1mm (¹⁄₂₀in) outside the edge of the embroidery. Use matching sewing thread, and work up the sides and along the upper edges of the embroidery, leaving the bottom edge open.

2a ▷ Take the corresponding pieces of plastic canvas cut from the templates provided and put them between the layers of fabric, making sure they fit properly, e.g. the gable walls fit into the embroidered gables and the side walls between them. Sew along the bottom edge, effectively making a "sandwich", with the plastic canvas between two layers of fabric.

2b ▷ If you are mounting a different shaped piece, such as a base, do not sew around all the sides but make sure you leave enough room at the bottom edge to push the plastic between the layers of fabric.

3 ▷ The embroidery should now be firmly stretched over the plastic shapes, but you will need to deal with the fabric margins. Trim all around the embroidery, leaving a margin of fabric at least 1.3cm (½in) on all sides, but trim the interfacing close to the back stitching on the wrong side.

Fold the fabric margin to the inside, and stitch it down, snipping carefully into angles and folding gable tops one side over the other, so that the plastic point will not work through the fabric. If you wish, you can mix the methods used to mount the embroidery on the plastic canvas pieces. For example, you could sandwich the walls as they form an awkward shape, and lace the roof, which is a simple rectangular shape.

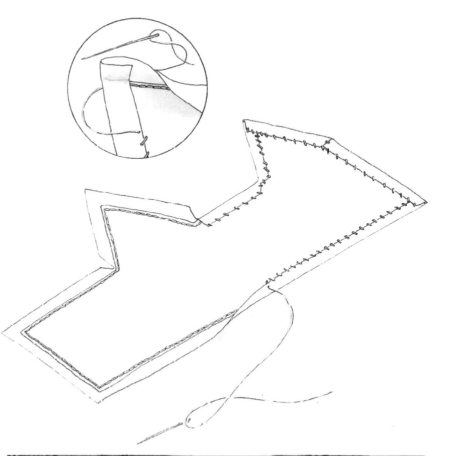

Assembling the cottage

1 ▽ Whichever method you choose for mounting the embroidery on the plastic canvas, the walls and roof are assembled in the same way as for the scented town houses, described on page 13. Bend the walls around and ladder stitch the side seam, then sew the roof to the walls.

2 The base is stitched to the rest of the house as described on page 25.

The Village Store

This store and the following shop form a pair, with the same roofs and bases, but they may be made as individual pieces if you wish. Many village shops have had to close, but some general stores remain open and villages attractive to tourists often boast craft shops.

DMC	Anchor
699	923
701	227
890	1044
349	13
704	256
738	942
814	45
318	399
310	black
922	1003
746	386
743	305
352	9
801	359
367	210
977	1002
906	256
783	307
938	380
351	10

Back stitch

DMC	Anchor
310	black
890	1044
801	359
704	256
701	227
436	1045
922	1003
743	305
367	210

French/Bullion knots

DMC	Anchor
349	13
704	256
922	1003
746	386
743	305
352	9
906	256
741	314

Measurements

The finished size of the store is 6.8cm tall, 9.4cm wide and 8.6cm deep (2⅝ x 3¾ x 3⅜in).

Materials

• *For the walls and awning*: Piece of cream 18-count Aida measuring 26 x 14cm (10¼ x 5½in)

• *For the roof*: Piece of dark green 28-count Jobelan evenweave measuring 12 x 14cm (4¾ x 5½in)

• *For the base*: Piece of light brown 28-count Jobelan evenweave measuring 13.5 x 12.5cm (5⅜ x 5in)

walls

overlap design from this point ▷

N.B. You will need a piece of interfacing the same size as the embroidery fabric for each piece of stitching you mount using the sandwich method.

- Piece of felt in a neutral colour, such as fawn or dark green, measuring 11 x 8.5cm (4½ x 3⅜in)
- DMC or Anchor stranded embroidery cotton in the colours shown on the charts
- Piece of 7-mesh plastic canvas measuring 22 x 14cm (8¾ x 5½in)
- Tapestry needle size 26 or 28
- Sewing needle
- Matching sewing thread
- Embroidery frame if required

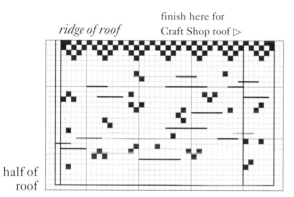

ridge of roof

finish here for Craft Shop roof ▷

half of roof

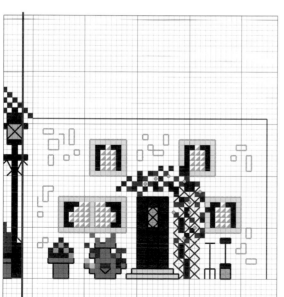

◁ overlap design from this point

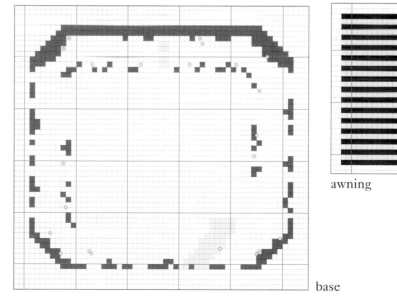

base

awning

890/Anchor 1044, but outline the name using one strand only. You may change the shop's name. Draw out the space for the lettering on a piece of graph paper, using one square for each stitch, and draw in the chosen name. Work this in place of the name on the chart.

Work bullion knots to represent runner beans, carrots and bananas, following the instructions given on page 112. Use two strands of thread, and wind them five or six times around the needle depending on the length of the knot.

The French knots are also worked using two strands of thread – the knots represent cauliflowers, sprouts, oranges, apples and flowers. The more times you wind the thread around the needle, the larger will be the finished knot. Make sure your apples and oranges are larger than your sprouts.

Work the awning following the separate chart.

Working the roof

Sew the roof on the dark green Jobelan, following the separate chart. The two sides of the roof are identical, so the chart shows only one side. Mark the centre, and stitch the centre ridge line first, making sure your stitching will be positioned with a margin of at least 2cm (¾ in) around it on all sides. Stitch the roof pattern below the centre ridge, then turn the work around and stitch the same pattern on the other side of the ridge. All the back stitching on the roof is worked using DMC 310/Anchor black and each stitch of the chart is worked over two threads of the fabric.

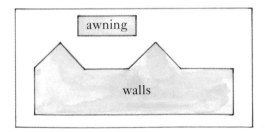

To work the embroidery

Sew the walls and awning on the cream Aida. Prepare the fabric as described in the techniques section, on page 109, marking the areas to be sewn with basting stitches and leaving a margin around each piece. Position the areas of sewing as shown in the diagram below. Begin sewing in the middle of the design, judged by eye.

Follow the chart for the walls on pages 28 and 29, working each of the cross stitches shown over one square of the fabric, using one strand of thread at a time. Work half cross stitches in the windows and for the basket in the front shop window. Work all the cross stitches before you begin the French knots and the back stitching.

All the stonework on the walls is back stitched using one strand of DMC 436/Anchor 1045. Work the remaining back stitch in the colours indicated.

Work the shop name using two strands of DMC

Working the base

The base is stitched on the light brown Jobelan following the separate chart. Prepare the fabric in the same way as for the roof, and work each cross stitch over two threads of fabric. Use two strands of thread together for the French knots, and wind them at least twice around the needle. Place them randomly around the shop if you prefer.

Wash and dry the pieces as explained in the techniques section, page 110.

Assembling the store

Cut the plastic walls, roof, base and awning from the piece of plastic canvas, using the templates given below. Separate the fabric walls from the awning, making sure there is sufficient margin around each piece. Mount the pieces using either the lacing or sandwich method (see pages 12 and 26). Cover the underside of the awning with felt.

The walls and roof of the store are assembled in the same way as the scented town houses, described on page 13. Ladder stitch the side seam in the walls, and add the awning before you sew on the roof. Ladder stitch the awning just above the shop name, and the thickness of the piece will hold it at an angle to the wall.

Sew the roof to the walls, making sure the overhang is equal on both sides, and that the top of the gables fits into the ridge of the roof.

Join the shop to the base, as described for the Flint Cottage, on page 25. Position it so that the paths are in front of the doors, and sew or stick felt to the underside of the base, covering all the internal stitching.

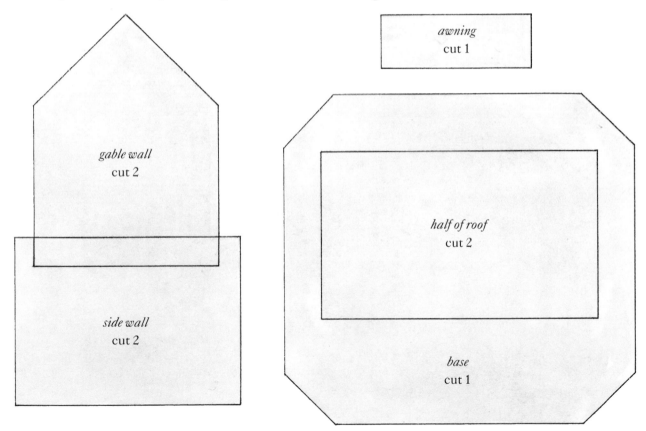

gable wall
cut 2

side wall
cut 2

awning
cut 1

half of roof
cut 2

base
cut 1

The Spinning Wheel Craft Shop

Village craft shops often sell the work of local craftsmen in rural areas. It is possible to find unique and beautiful pieces at such places. With its hobby horse and spinning wheel, this craft shop obviously features pieces made by a woodworker.

walls

	DMC	Anchor		DMC	Anchor	Back stitch		French knots	
	415	398		739	1009	**DMC**	**Anchor**	**DMC**	**Anchor**
	310	black		938	380	310	black	310	black
	613	853		905	257	920	1004	986	246
	775	975		890	1044	938	380	977	1002
	972	298		977	1002	817	46	817	46
	433	371		920	1004	890	1044		
	809	130		702	226	702	226		
	986	246		369	1043	433	371		
	3790	898				3790	898		
						436	1045		

Measurements

The finished size of the craft shop is 7.6cm tall, 9.4cm wide and 8.6cm deep (3 x 3¾ x 3⅜in).

Materials

- *For the walls*: Piece of antique white 18-count Aida measuring 24 x 12cm (9½ x 4¾in)
- *For the roof*: Piece of dark green 28-count Jobelan evenweave measuring 10 x 16cm (4 x 6⅜in)
- *For the base*: Piece of light brown 28-count Jobelan evenweave measuring 13.5 x 12.5cm (5⅜ x 5in)

N.B. You will need a piece of interfacing the same size as the embroidery fabric for each piece of stitching you mount using the sandwich method.

- Piece of felt in a neutral colour, such as fawn or dark green, measuring 9.3 x 8.5cm (3¾ x 3⅜in)
- DMC or Anchor stranded embroidery cotton in the colours shown on the chart
- Piece of 7-mesh plastic canvas measuring 20 x 14cm (8 x 5½in)
- Tapestry needle size 26 or 28
- Sewing needle
- Matching sewing thread
- Embroidery frame if required

To work the embroidery

Sew the shop walls first. Preparing the Aida fabric as described in the techniques section, page 109. Mark the outline of the walls on the fabric with basting stitches, leaving a margin of at least 2cm (¾in) on all sides. The irregular shape will not have an obvious centre, but begin stitching in the middle of the fabric judged by eye.

Following the chart given for the walls on page 32, work each cross stitch over one square of the fabric. Use one strand of thread throughout, except for the French knots, the lettering and spinning wheel which are stitched using two strands of thread together. Work all the cross stitches before you begin working the French knots and back stitching.

All the stonework is worked using DMC 436/Anchor 1045. Work the remaining back stitch in the colours indicated on the chart.

Outline the shop name on the front wall and the craft shop sign on the side wall using one strand of

DMC 938/Anchor 380, but work all the lettering using two strands. Change the name of this shop if you wish by following the instructions on page 30.

The symbol on the craft shop sign represents embroidery in a hoop and is outlined using DMC 310/Anchor Black.

French knots are used to suggest flowers and foliage. Follow the chart for the position of the knots, and use two strands of thread together. Wind the threads at least twice around the needle to give a raised effect. The eye of the hobby horse in the front window is also worked with a French knot, but use only one strand and wind it once around the needle.

Working the roof

Stitch the roof on the dark green Jobelan, following the chart given for the roof of the Village

Store on page 29. The Craft Shop roof is slightly smaller and the area to be worked is shown on the chart. Mark the area to be stitched, leaving a margin all around it as described in the techniques section, page 109. All the back stitching on the roof is worked using DMC 310/Anchor Black and each stitch of the chart is worked over two threads of the fabric.

Working the base

Stitch the base on the light brown Jobelan, following the chart for the base of the Village Store on page 29, but work the pathways using DMC 613/Anchor 853, the grass using DMC 702/Anchor 226 and the French knots using DMC 977/Anchor 1002. Use two strands of thread together for the French knots, and wind them at least twice around the needle. Scatter the knots randomly around the shop. Work each stitch over two threads of the fabric.

When all the embroidery has been completed, wash and dry the pieces as explained in the techniques section, page 110.

Assembling the shop

Cut the pieces for the walls, roof and base from the plastic canvas, using the templates below. Follow the instructions given on page 31 for assembling the Village Store, but omit the details for adding the awning.

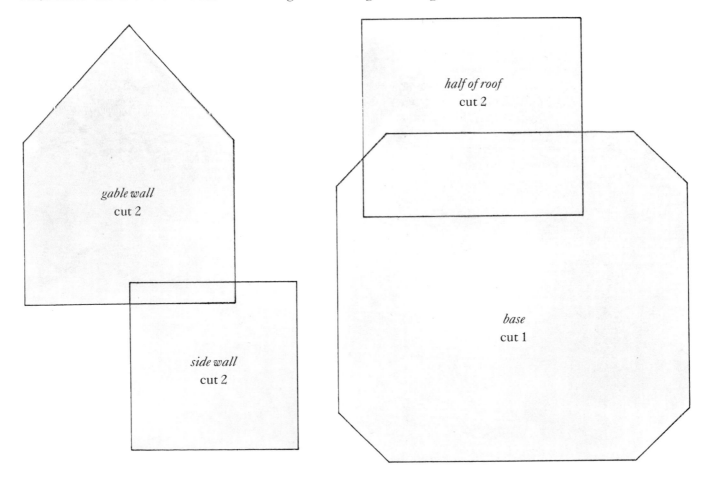

gable wall
cut 2

side wall
cut 2

half of roof
cut 2

base
cut 1

The Bothy – A Thatched Cottage

Many people dream of retiring to a cottage like this, to live out their days in peace and serenity. There are numerous examples scattered all over the countryside to tempt you.

DMC	Anchor
318	399
745	300
743	305
310	black
905	257
3371	382
3031	381
895	269
988	257
986	246
613	853
961	76
340	118
612	888
3790	898

Back stitch

DMC	Anchor
310	black
895	269
3031	381
318	399

French knots

DMC	Anchor
743	305
760	1002
961	76
340	118

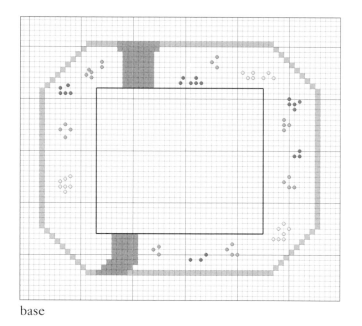

base

walls

overlap design from this point ▷

Measurements

The finished size of The Bothy is 6.5cm tall, 9.8cm wide and 8.2cm deep (2⅝ x 3⅞ x 3¼in).

Materials

- *For the walls and roof*: Piece of cream 18-count Aida measuring 37.5 x 15.5cm (14¾ x 6⅛in)
- *For the base*: Piece of green 28-count Jobelan evenweave measuring 14 x 12.5cm (5½ x 5in)

N.B. You will need a piece of interfacing the same size as the embroidery fabric for each piece of stitching you mount using the sandwich method.

- Piece of felt in a neutral colour, such as fawn or dark green, measuring 10 x 8cm (4 x 3¼in)
- DMC or Anchor stranded embroidery cotton in the colours shown on the charts
- Piece of 7-mesh plastic canvas measuring 20.5 x 13.5cm (8⅛ x 5⅜in)
- Tapestry needle size 26 or 28
- Sewing needle
- Matching sewing thread
- Embroidery frame if required

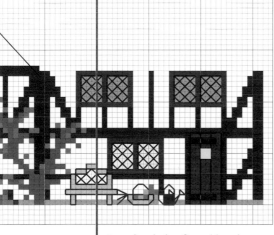

◁ overlap design from this point

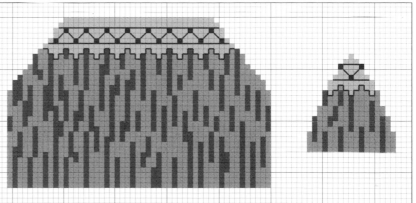

ridge of roof

half of roof

hip

To work the embroidery

Sew the walls and roof on the cream Aida. Prepare the fabric as described in the techniques section, page 109, marking the areas to be stitched with basting stitches and leaving a margin around each piece. The diagram shows how to place the pieces on the fabric. Begin sewing each piece in the middle of the design as far as possible.

Sew the walls first, following the chart on pages 36 and 37. Work each cross stitch over one square of the fabric. Use one strand of thread at a time, except for the French knots which are worked using two strands. Work all the cross stitches before the back stitches and French knots. Work all the back stitch in the colours indicated on the charts. Some back stitches are worked over two or more squares, so follow the chart carefully.

Work the French knots using two strands of thread, and wind them at least twice around the needle. The roses are worked using DMC 760/Anchor1022, and the flowers on the shrub on the gable wall using DMC 743/Anchor 305.

Working the roof

After completing the walls, sew the roof pieces: one main roof and two hips. Following the chart on page 37 which shows half the main roof, sew the centre ridge line, and work the pattern below it. Then turn your work round and sew the same pattern on the other side of the centre ridge line.

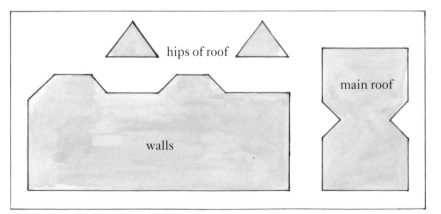

All the back stitching on the roof is worked using DMC 3031/Anchor 381.

Working the base

Using the green Jobelan fabric and following the chart on page 36, work each cross stitch over two threads of the fabric. Place the French knots randomly in groups to resemble a flower garden.

Assembling the cottage

1 Cut out the walls, roof and base from the plastic canvas, using the templates opposite. Separate the fabric walls from the roof pieces, making sure there is sufficient margin around each piece. Mount the pieces – you will probably find it easier to mount the roof pieces using the sandwich method on page 26, as the roof hips are so small.

2 The walls of the cottage are assembled in the same way as for the Scented Town Houses given on page 13. Begin by sewing the side seam in the walls to make the cottage shape.

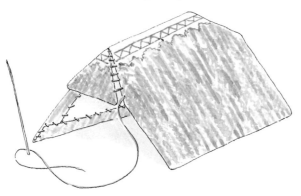

3 △ Assemble the roof by bending the main piece along the ridge, then ladder stitch the two roof hips in position at either end.

4 Ladder stitch the roof to the walls, as described for the Scented Town Houses, making sure the overhang is equal on all sides and that the gables fit under the hips of the roof.

5 Join the cottage to the base, as described for the Flint Cottage on page 25, positioning the base so that the paths lead directly to the doors. Sew or stick felt to the underside of the base to cover all the internal stitching.

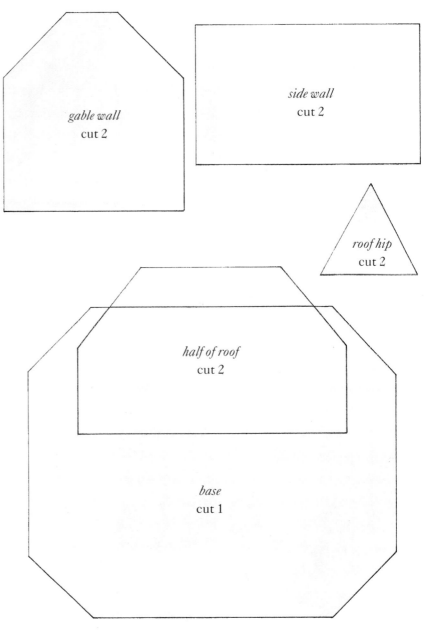

gable wall
cut 2

side wall
cut 2

roof hip
cut 2

half of roof
cut 2

base
cut 1

The Hall – A Small Country House

This house may originally have been someone's weekend retreat. The pointed windows suggest that it originated from the first half of the nineteenth century, but modern-day owners will have made sure that the plumbing dates from a much later period.

ridge of roof

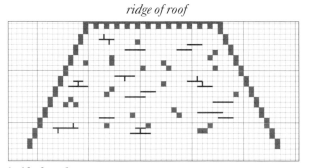

half of roof

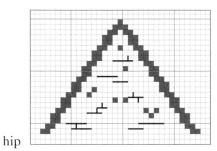

hip

DMC	Anchor
415	398
414	400
413	236
762	234
3608	86
3350	69
818	271
906	256
904	258
988	257
341	117
340	118
3746	1030
793	176

Back stitch

DMC	Anchor
413	236
414	400

French knots

DMC	Anchor
3350+818	69+271
904+413	258+236
3746	1030

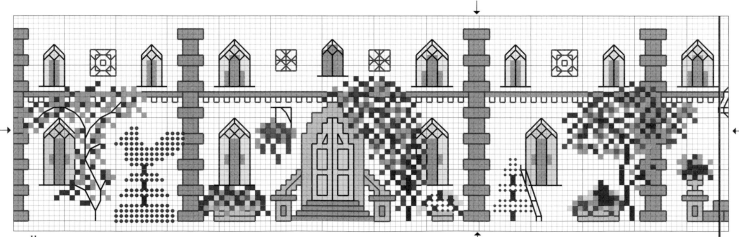

walls

overlap design from this point ▷

Measurements

The finished size of the Hall is 8.5cm tall, 12.2cm wide and 11cm deep (3⅜ x 4¾ x 4⅜in).

Materials

- *For the walls*: Piece of antique white 18-count Aida measuring 30 x 10cm (11¾ x 4in)
- *For the roof*: Piece of medium dark grey 28-count Minster linen measuring 23.5 x 14cm (9¼ x 5½in)
- *For the base*: Piece of green 28-count Jobelan evenweave measuring 16.5 x 15.5cm (6½ x 6⅛in)

N.B. You will need a piece of interfacing the same size as the embroidery fabric for each piece of stitching you mount using the sandwich method.

- Piece of felt in a neutral colour, such as fawn or dark green, measuring 12 x 11cm (4¾ x 4⅜in)
- DMC or Anchor stranded embroidery cotton in the colours shown on the charts
- Piece of 7-mesh plastic canvas measuring 21.5 x 21.5cm (8½ x 8½in)
- Tapestry needle size 26 or 28
- Sewing needle
- Matching sewing thread
- Embroidery frame if required

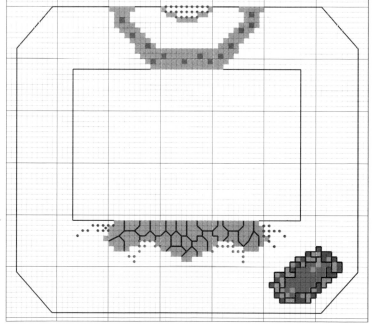

base

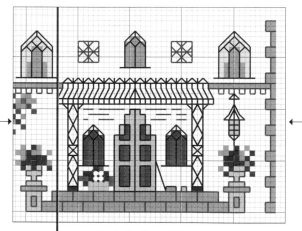

◁ overlap design from this point

To work the embroidery

Sew the walls onto the antique white Aida. Prepare the fabric as described in the techniques section, page 109, marking the areas to be stitched with basting stitches and leaving a margin around each piece. Begin sewing at the centre of the design. Work each cross stitch shown on the chart on pages 40 and 41 over one square of the fabric, and use one strand of thread for all the cross stitches and back stitches. Complete all the cross stitching before working the back stitching and French knots.

Work all the back stitch in the colours indicated on the charts. Some back stitches are worked over two or more squares, so follow the chart carefully.

Work the topiary by placing French knots close together to resemble foliage. Use one strand of DMC 413/Anchor 236, and one strand of DMC 904/Anchor 258 in the needle together, and wind the threads at least twice around the needle. You do not need to work the exact number of knots shown on the chart, just the general shape.

The remaining French knots are worked using one strand of DMC 3350/Anchor 69, and one strand of DMC 818/Anchor 271 together.

Working the roof

Sew the roof designs on the grey Minster linen, following the charts on page 40. First mark the areas to be stitched as shown in the diagram. One half of the main roof is shown on the chart. Work the centre ridge line, and the pattern below it. Then turn the fabric round and work the same pattern on the other side of the centre ridge line. Work the two roof hips. All the back stitching is worked using DMC 413/Anchor 236, and each stitch is worked over two threads of the fabric.

Working the base

The base is sewn onto the green Jobelan fabric.

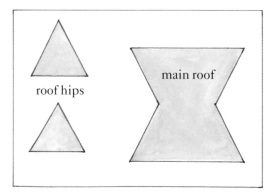

roof hips

main roof

Prepare the fabric as before. Follow the chart on page 41 and work each stitch over two threads of the fabric. Work the mauve French knots using two strands of DMC 3746/Anchor 1030, and work the pink ones using one strand of DMC 3350/Anchor 69 and one strand of DMC 818/Anchor 271 together in the needle. The back stitching is worked using DMC 413/Anchor 236.

Wash and dry the pieces as described in the techniques section, page 110.

Assembling the hall

1 Using the templates opposite, cut out the walls, roof pieces and base from the plastic canvas. Mount the embroidery on the plastic pieces using either construction method (see pages 12 and 26) – you may find it may be easier to mount the roof using the sandwich method.

2 Assemble the walls in the same way as for the Scented Town Houses, described on page 13.

3 △ Assemble the roof as shown in the diagram. Bend the two sides of the main roof downwards at the centre ridge, and ladder stitch the hips between the sides.

4 Place the roof on top of the walls, making sure the overhang is equal on all sides. Ladder stitch the two pieces together all around the top of the walls, checking the overhang as you go.

5 Join the Hall to the base, as described for the Flint Cottage on page 25. Position it so that the crazy paving terrace is beside the verandah at the back of the house. Sew or stick felt to the underside of the base to cover all the internal stitching.

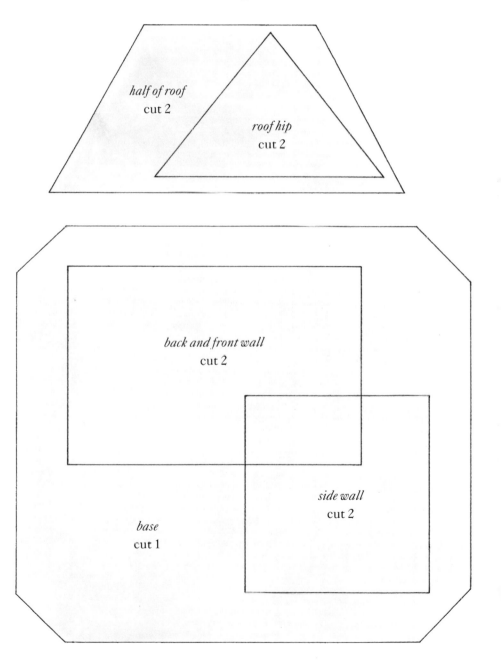

half of roof
cut 2

roof hip
cut 2

back and front wall
cut 2

side wall
cut 2

base
cut 1

The Swan Inn

The distinctive half-timbered appearance of the inn suggests that it is probably one of the oldest buildings in the village. Perhaps it was once a coaching inn. This piece is more challenging than a simple cottage shape, but the results will be well worth your time and effort.

DMC	Anchor
310	black
791	123
498	100
809	130
301	349
644	830
415	398
blanc	white
3747	117
801	359

DMC	Anchor
648	900
3031	381
977	1002
895	246
783	307
904	258
906	256
3825	1047
987	210

Back stitch

DMC	Anchor
310	black
3031	381
648	900
895	246
791	123
3825	1047
301	349

French knots

DMC	Anchor
310	black
498	1006
blanc	white

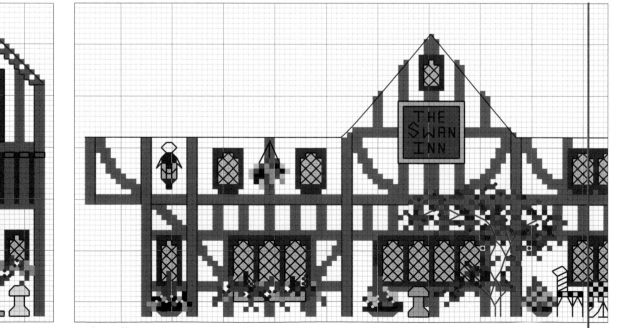

front wall

main walls

overlap design from this point ▷

Measurements

The finished size of the Inn is 8cm tall, 12.2cm wide and 11cm deep (3¼ x 4¾ x 4⅜in).

Materials

- *For the main and front walls*: Piece of cream 18-count Aida measuring 40 x 12cm (15¾ x 4¾in)
- *For the roofs*: Piece of dark brown 28-count Jobelan evenweave measuring 23 x 14cm (9⅛ x 5½in)
- *For the base*: Piece of light grey 28-count Jobelan evenweave measuring 16.5 x 15.5cm (6½ x 6⅛in)

N.B. You will need a piece of interfacing the same size as the embroidered fabric for each piece mounted using the sandwich method.

- Piece of felt in a neutral colour, such as fawn or dark green, measuring 12 x 11cm (4¾ x 4⅜in)
- DMC or Anchor stranded embroidery cotton in the colours shown on the charts
- Piece of 7-mesh plastic canvas measuring 25.5 x 20cm (10 x 8in)
- Tapestry needle size 26 or 28
- Sewing needle
- Matching sewing thread
- Embroidery frame if required

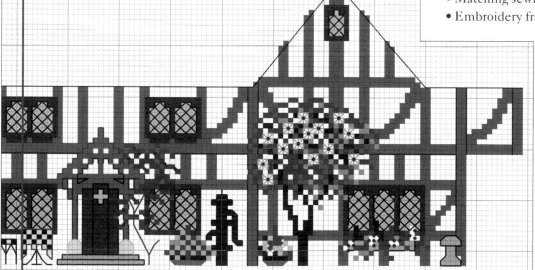

◁ overlap design from this point

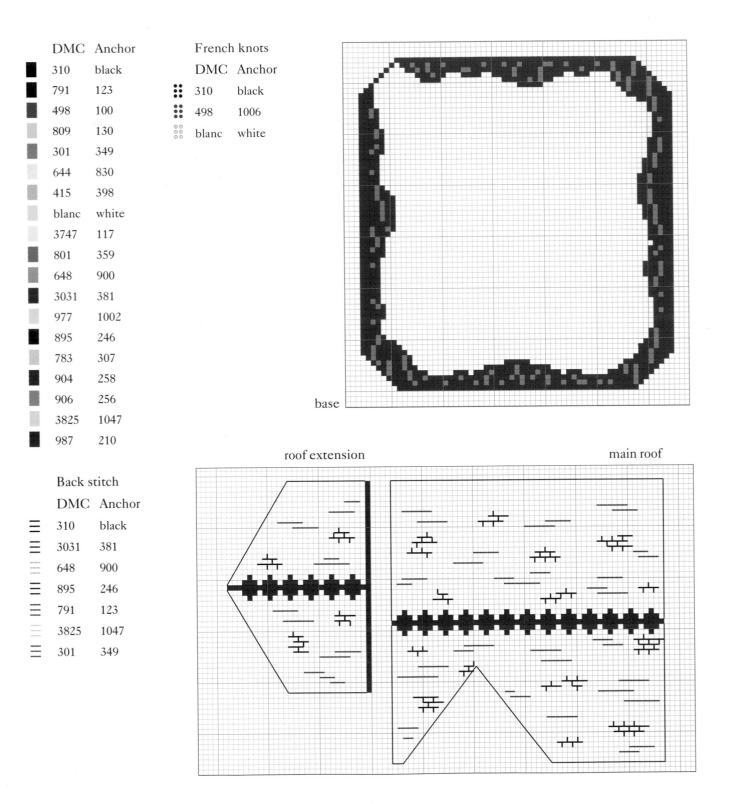

DMC   Anchor

■ 310   black
■ 791   123
■ 498   100
■ 809   130
■ 301   349
■ 644   830
■ 415   398
■ blanc   white
■ 3747   117
■ 801   359
■ 648   900
■ 3031   381
■ 977   1002
■ 895   246
■ 783   307
■ 904   258
■ 906   256
■ 3825   1047
■ 987   210

French knots
DMC   Anchor
310   black
498   1006
blanc   white

Back stitch
DMC   Anchor
310   black
3031   381
648   900
895   246
791   123
3825   1047
301   349

base

roof extension   main roof

To work the embroidery

Sew the walls onto the cream Aida. Prepare the fabric by marking the areas for sewing with basting stitches, as described in the techniques section on page 109, leaving a margin of at least 2cm (¾in) around all sides of the front and main walls, as shown in the diagram below.

Begin sewing in the middle of each section of the walls judged by eye, and work each of the cross stitches shown on the charts on pages 44 and 45 over one square of the fabric, using one strand of thread for the cross stitches. Work all the cross stitches before you begin the back stitches and French knots.

Work all the back stitch in the colours indicated on the charts. Some back stitches are worked over two or more squares, so follow the chart carefully.

The centre of each back-stitched flower on the tree is a small French knot. Use two strands of thread but keep the knots small by winding the thread only once or twice around the needle.

Work the name of the inn using two strands of DMC 310/Anchor black. If you wish to change the name, follow the instructions in the Village Store on page 30. Remember to change the picture on the inn sign to match.

Work the swan's eye as a small French knot using one strand once around the needle.

The remaining French knots, representing flowers, are worked using two strands of thread together. Wind them twice or more around the needle to give the required size of flower.

Working the roofs

Sew the roofs on the brown Jobelan fabric, following the charts on page 46. Work one main roof and one roof extension. Mark the areas to be sewn, leaving a margin around each piece and spacing the areas of stitching as shown in the diagram below.

All the back stitching on the roof is worked over two threads of the fabric.

Working the base

The base is sewn on the grey Jobelan fabric following the chart on page 46. Prepare the fabric as before, then work each cross stitch over two threads of the fabric.

Wash and dry the pieces as described in the techniques section, page 110.

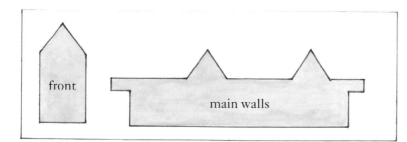

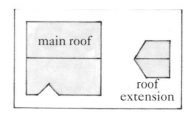

Assembling the inn

1 ▷ Cut out the plastic canvas pieces, using the templates given on page 49. There are five different shaped walls for the main piece, and three different pieces for the front of the inn, including the jetty, the part which hangs out over the front door. The roof is made up of four pieces, and the base is one piece only.

Separate the front of the inn from the main walls, with a margin of about 2cm (¾in) around each piece. Mount the walls using the sandwich method because of the awkward shape (see page 26). Sew along the bottom edge so that the plastic pieces can be pushed in from the top.

Next mount the upper front and lower front with the jetty in between. When you turn the margins to the inside, stretch the fabric tightly over the plastic. The walls will be bent into an "L" shape with an internal corner, and any spare fabric will bunch at this point.

2 ▽ Sew the front to the main walls. Bend the front so that the upper part overhangs the lower, and bend the main walls into an "L" shape, with the two side walls pointing forwards. Place the front between the side walls, fitting the jetty along the side edges as shown in the diagram. The front gable stands above the side edges.

Ladder stitch the two pieces together, taking small stitches and drawing the pieces together by pulling smoothly on the thread. When you negotiate the jetty, leave some of the stitches loose until you are around the corner, then draw them up.

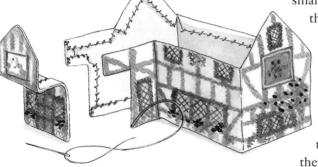

If you are not satisfied with the seams, work extra cross stitches on them using DMC 3031/Anchor 381, or sew a piece of narrow braid over them. This will look like an extra beam, and will not spoil the appearance of your work.

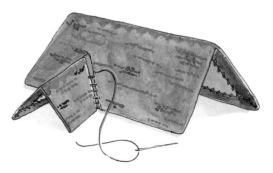

3 △ Separate the embroidered main roof from the roof extension and mount them on the plastic pieces using your preferred construction method (see pages 12 and 26). Sew the roof extension to the main roof as shown in the diagram.

Place the roof on top of the walls, making sure the front piece fits over the front gable and the overhang is equal on all sides. Ladder stitch the walls to the roof.

4 Sew the inn to the base as described on page 25, and sew or stick felt to the underside of the base to cover all the internal stitching.

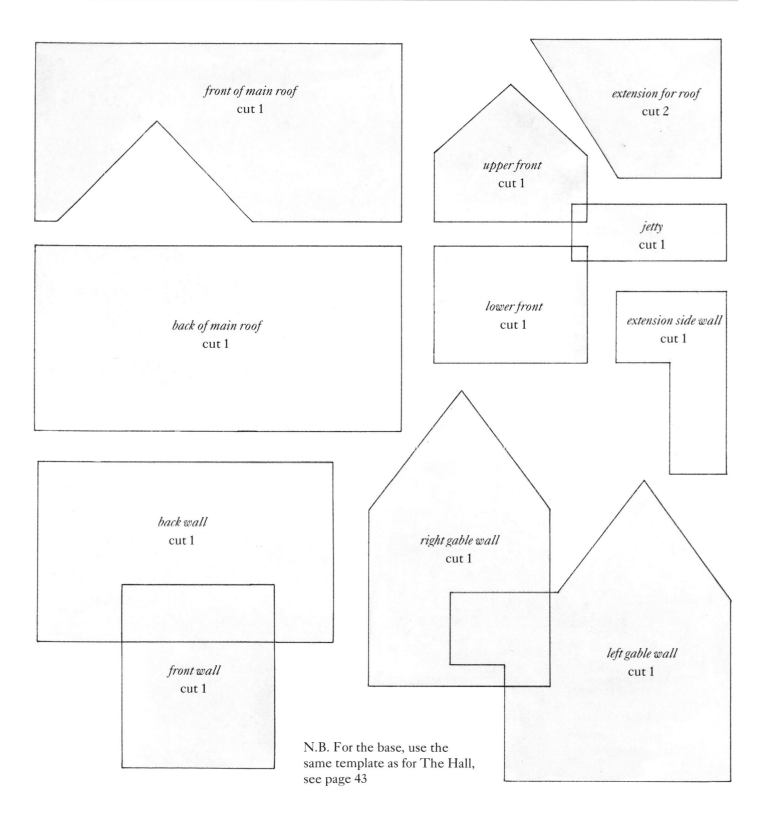

front of main roof
cut 1

extension for roof
cut 2

upper front
cut 1

jetty
cut 1

back of main roof
cut 1

lower front
cut 1

extension side wall
cut 1

back wall
cut 1

right gable wall
cut 1

front wall
cut 1

left gable wall
cut 1

N.B. For the base, use the same template as for The Hall, see page 43

The Parish Church

*Is there an old stone church like this near you? They may be found all over the country in
towns and villages. Do stop to look around if you have the time – you may be inspired by
the beautiful architecture and stained glass.*

DMC	Anchor
415	398
317	400
318	399
3747	117
310	black
760	1022
986	246
791	123
743	305

DMC	Anchor
905	257
809	130
702	226
644	830
844	1041
334	977
500	879
815	43
Madeira gold	

Back stitch

DMC	Anchor
317	400
310	black
Madeira gold	
844	1041
986	246
815	43

French/Bullion knots

DMC	Anchor
349	13
310	black
906+986	256+246
815	43

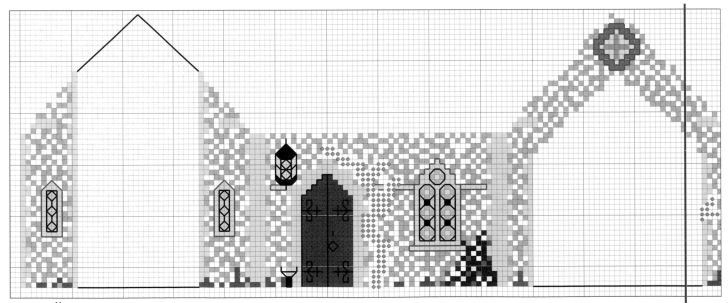

nave walls

overlap design from this point ▷

Measurements

The finished size of The Church is 9.5cm tall, 18.8cm long and 10.6cm deep (3¾ x 7⅜ x 4¼in).

Materials

- *For the walls of the tower, nave and chancel*: Piece of antique white 18-count Aida measuring 37 x 26cm (14 ½ x 10¼in)
- *For the roofs*: Piece of medium grey 28-count Jobelan evenweave measuring 17 x 28cm (6¾ x 11in)
- *For the base*: Piece of green 28-count Jobelan evenweave measuring 15 x 24cm (6 x 9½in)

N.B. You will need a piece of interfacing the same size as the embroidery fabric for each piece of stitching you mount using the sandwich method.

- Piece of felt in a neutral colour, such as fawn or dark green, measuring 19 x 10.5cm (7½ x 4¼in)
- DMC or Anchor stranded embroidery cotton in the colours shown on the charts
- Madeira metallic thread no. 40, colour gold 7
- Piece of 7-mesh plastic canvas measuring 35 x 22cm (13⅞ x 8¾in)
- Tapestry needle size 26 or 28
- Sewing needle
- Matching sewing thread
- Embroidery frame if required

ridge of roof ←   area of chancel roof   →

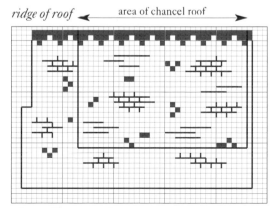

chancel/nave roof

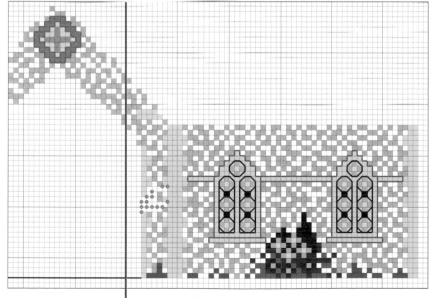

◁ overlap design from this point

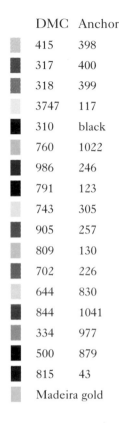

DMC	Anchor
415	398
317	400
318	399
3747	117
310	black
760	1022
986	246
791	123
743	305
905	257
809	130
702	226
644	830
844	1041
334	977
500	879
815	43
	Madeira gold

Back stitch

DMC	Anchor
317	400
310	black
	Madeira gold
844	1041
986	246
815	43

chancel walls

tower walls

French/Bullion knots			French/Bullion knots	
DMC	Anchor		DMC	Anchor
349	13		906+986	256+246
310	black		815	43

To work the embroidery

The church walls are made up of three pieces sewn separately, the tower, the nave and the chancel. When the sewing is finished and mounted on plastic canvas, the pieces are sewn together to make the church. Sew the walls on the antique white Aida, marking the three areas with basting stitches, as described in the techniques section, page 109. Position the pieces on the fabric as shown in the diagram opposite, with a margin of at least 2cm (¾in), around each piece.

Begin to sew each piece at the centre of the design, judged by eye, following the charts on page 50 to 51 and 52. Work each stitch over one square of the fabric. The charts show parts of the tower and nave left blank where they are joined together and no stitching would be visible. Most of this design is sewn using one strand of thread at a time, but the gold figures on the clock and some of the French knots use two threads together.

Work all the cross stitches before the back stitching and French knots. Work all the back stitch in the colours indicated on the charts. Some back stitches are worked over two or more squares, so follow the chart carefully.

The creepers around the church walls are represented by French knots stitched closely together. Use one strand each of DMC 986/Anchor 246 and DMC 906/Anchor 256 together in the needle, and wind the threads at least twice around the needle for each knot.

The red berries on the yew against the chancel wall are worked using two strands. Do not make these too large!

The eye of the pecking bird on the tower wall is made from a tiny French knot. Use one strand , and wind the thread once round the needle.

Work the grapes on the "stained glass" window in the same way using one strand.

Work the "love-lies-bleeding" flowers on the back wall of the chancel as bullion knots, using

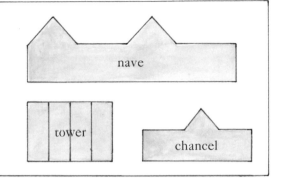

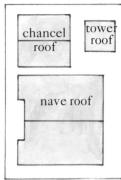

two strands of DMC 814/Anchor 45, and following the instructions on page 112.

Working the roofs

Sew the roofs on the grey Jobelan fabric, following the chart on page 51. Work one nave roof and one chancel roof. Mark the areas to be stitched, leaving a margin around each piece and spacing the areas of stitching as shown in the diagram above. There is one chart given for both roofs. The design for the chancel roof is part of the nave roof design, as marked on the chart.

The sides of each roof are the same, so work the centre ridge line, work the relevant chart below it then turn the fabric round and work the same design on the other side of the centre ridge line.

All the back stitching on the roof is worked using DMC 317/Anchor 400, and each stitch of the chart is worked over two threads of the fabric.

Make the roof for the tower by covering the plastic canvas tower roof with grey Jobelan fabric. Back stitch a few lines on it using DMC 317/Anchor 400.

Wash and dry the fabric as explained in the techniques section, page 110.

Working the base

The base is made from the green Jobelan fabric, but you will not need to make it until the church has been assembled.

Assembling the church

1 Cut out the plastic canvas pieces for the church using the templates given on page 55. Check carefully that all pieces are cut correctly.

Tower: 4 walls, 1 roof.
Nave: 2 gable walls, 2 side walls, 2 roof pieces.
Chancel: 1 gable wall, 2 side walls, 2 roof pieces.
Base: 1 piece

2▽ Separate the tower, nave and chancel by cutting carefully between them, making sure you leave a margin of at least 2cm (¾in) around each piece. The parts of the tower and chancel left blank **must not be removed** but left as part of the walls. Mount the chancel and nave on the plastic canvas pieces using the method you prefer. The tower must be mounted using the lacing method because the top of the stitching folds over the plastic to resemble the inner side of the tower, as shown in the diagram. Fold in the sides first and lace horizontally, then fold in the top and bottom and lace these sides vertically.

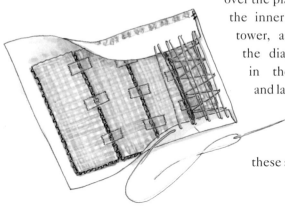

3 To make the nave, bend the four walls around so that the side edges meet, then ladder stitch the side seam to close.

4▷ Sew one side of the tower to the end gable wall of the nave, matching the blank areas shown on the chart.

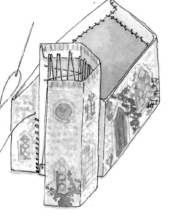

5▷Before you sew the side seam in the tower, place the tower roof just below the stitching on the inside of the tower, and sew it to the walls. As you go, the tower walls will bend round, and the side edges will meet together. Ladder stitch the side seam in the tower as shown in the diagram.

6 Mount the roofs for the nave and chancel using the method you prefer. Sew the nave roof in position on top of the walls, with one side against the tower wall, where you will need to slip stitch the pieces together. If you find it difficult to work in this confined area, try gluing the roof against the tower using a fabric glue.

7 ◁ Sew the roof of the chancel to the walls with a slight overhang on the gable wall. Make sure it does not extend beyond the side walls.

8▷ Ladder stitch the chancel to the nave, working up the side wall, around the roof and down the remaining side. Use the blank area on the nave wall as a guide, and match up the creeper, which grows across the chancel wall and on to the nave.

9 Make the base and stitch the church to it. Mark the position of the base on the green Jobelan fabric. Stand the church on the fabric, and mark its position too. No chart is given and it may be left plain or you may sew French knots in random groups around the church. Choose suitable colours to represent flowers, and use two strands of thread together. Mount the embroidered base on the plastic canvas and ladder stitch the church to the base as described on page 25, checking as you go that the pieces remain in line. Sew or stick the felt to the underside of the base to cover any visible stitching.

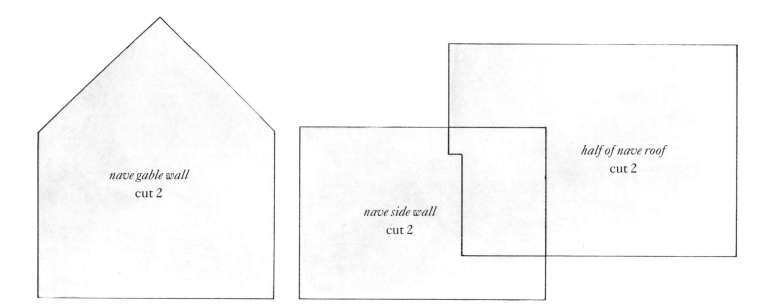

nave gable wall
cut 2

nave side wall
cut 2

half of nave roof
cut 2

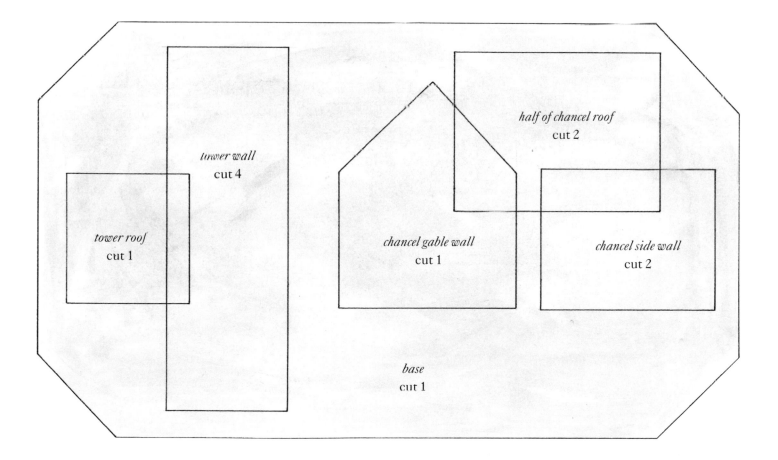

tower wall
cut 4

half of chancel roof
cut 2

tower roof
cut 1

chancel gable wall
cut 1

chancel side wall
cut 2

base
cut 1

KEEPSAKES

The projects in this section are practical as well as decorative, and include money boxes, trinket boxes, a clock – even a vase. Stitch them for yourself or make a special keepsake as a gift for a friend. Some of the pieces will take time to complete but others are quite small and would make ideal projects for busy stitchers wanting fast results.

Bird House Money Box

Here is a suitable money box for a nest egg! The slots in the roof will receive your savings, and a hatch in the base will let you get at the money when a rainy day looms.

Measurements

The finished size of the money box is 10.5cm tall, 9.8cm wide and 10cm deep (4¼ x 3⅞ x 4in).

Materials

Money boxes must be lined to prevent coins catching in the internal threads, so use the sandwich method, on page 26, to mount the stitching on the plastic pieces.

- *For the walls*: Piece of antique white 18-count Aida measuring 35 x 13.5cm (13¾ x 5⅜in)
- Same-sized piece of interfacing
- *For the roof:* Piece of medium green 18-count Aida measuring 19 x 14cm (7½ x 5½in)
- Same-sized piece of interfacing
- *For the base*: Piece of medium green 18-count Aida measuring 14cm square (5½in square)
- Same-sized piece of interfacing – optional
- *For the base and the hatch:* Medium green felt measuring 15 x 13cm (6 x 5¼in)
- *To open the hatch*: Black tape 4cm (1½in) long, 5mm (¼in) wide
- *For the stays*: Interfacing or felt 17 x 9cm (6¾ x 3⅝in)
- Iron-on interfacing 6 x 5cm (2⅜ x 2in)
- DMC or Anchor stranded embroidery cotton in the colours shown on the charts
- 7-mesh plastic canvas measuring 24.5cm square (9¾in square)
- Tapestry needle size 26
- Sewing needle
- Matching sewing thread
- Embroidery frame if required

To work the embroidery

Prepare the fabric as described in the techniques section, on page 109, marking the outline of the bird house walls and the centre of the design on the antique white Aida fabric with basting stitches. Leave a margin of 2cm (¾in) around the shape of the walls on all sides, for mounting the fabric on the plastic. Begin to stitch at the centre of the design, and follow the chart given for the walls on pages 60 and 61. Use one strand of thread at a time, and work each cross stitch over one square of the fabric. Complete all the cross stitches before you begin the back stitch.

Back stitch following the chart for position and embroidery colours.

Working the roof

Stitch the roof on the rectangular piece of green Aida. Mark the area for the roof and the ridge, positioning the roof with a margin of 2cm (¾in) around it on all sides. Follow the instructions for making an opening in the fabric given in the techniques section, on page 109, for the money slots. Mark them with basting stitches and iron interfacing into the slots. The two sides of the roof are identical, so the chart for the roof shows only one side. When the first side is complete, turn the work around and stitch the same pattern on the other side of the roof, leaving a gap of one row of fabric squares between the two sides of the ridge. Use one strand of thread at a time, and work all the back stitching on the roof using DMC 561/Anchor 212.

Wash and dry the walls and roof as described in the techniques section, on page 110. The base will be made later when the walls and roof have been stitched together.

Cut out the plastic canvas pieces using the templates provided on page 63. Cut two side walls, two gable walls, a roof ridge, two roof pieces and a base from the plastic canvas. Cut the slots from the roof pieces and the hatch from the base. The piece removed from this hole is the right size for the hatch tray once the sides have been trimmed. Cut two hatch side pieces and one end, and stays for the hatch and slots.

The stays around the slots and hatch openings are not essential. If you are in a hurry you may omit them, but they help to strengthen the money box.

DMC	Anchor
562	208
561	212
3799	236
3756	1037
341	117
793	176
3072	234
792	177
3825	1047
413	401
744	301
743	305
3607	87
318	399
3609	85
3608	86
3747	117

Back stitch

DMC	Anchor
3799	236
318	399
792	177
3607	87
561	212
743	305
3825	1047

ridge of roof

half of roof

main walls

overlap design from this point ▷

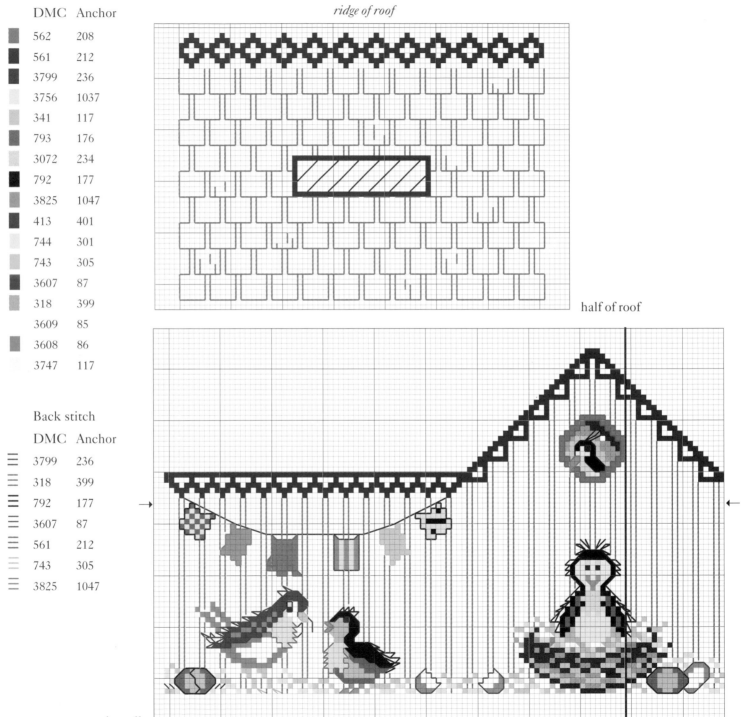

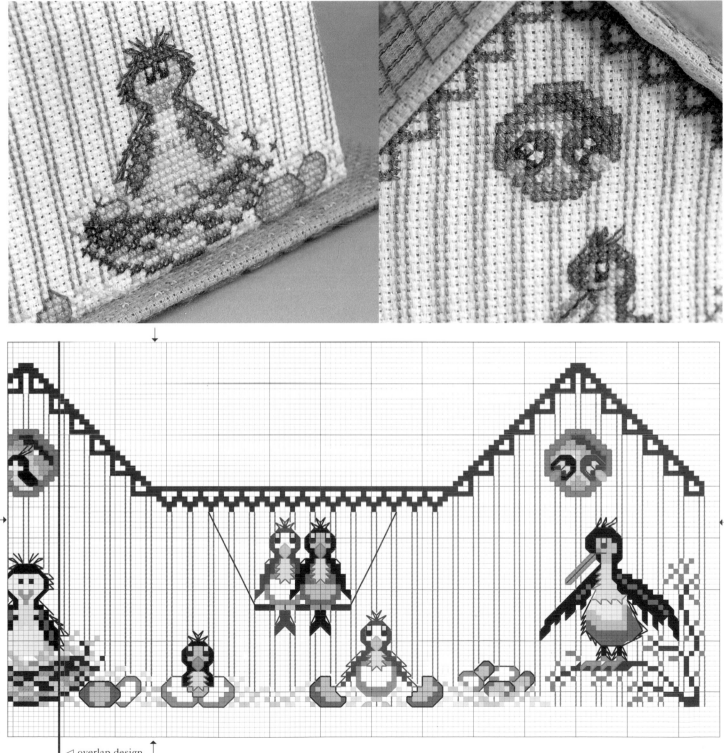

◁ overlap design
from this point

Assembling the money box

1 The money box is assembled in the same way as the houses in the Cross Stitch Village. Mount the walls on the plastic canvas using the sandwich method, described on page 26, and ladder stitch the side seam in the walls (see also page 13).

2 ▽ The roof has a centre ridge and two money slots. Mount the roof using the sandwich method, stitching the fabric to the interfacing along the top edge, down one side and along the bottom edge. Insert the roof pieces so that there is a gap between them, and sew up the remaining side. Fold the margins to the inside and stitch them to the interfacing. Fold the roof in half, and place the ridge piece between the fabric layers at the top of the roof. Stitch the ends of the ridge together and work a row of running stitches beneath it.

3 ◁ Make the slot openings and cover the stays as described in the techniques section on pages 109 to 110. Stitch the stays to the wrong side of the slots inside the roof.

4 Place the roof on top of the walls and stitch them together, as described on page 13.

5 Lay the plastic canvas base on the square of green Aida and mark the positions of the base and hatch. Iron interfacing to the area for the hatch opening. Stand the assembled bird house on the base over the hatch and mark the position of the walls. Work a random pattern of cross stitches between the walls and the edge of the base to represent straw, using DMC 743/Anchor 305 and DMC 744/Anchor 301. Use one strand of thread at a time.

6 When the embroidery is complete, wash and dry the fabric and mount it on the plastic canvas base using the lacing or sandwich methods. Follow the instructions given in the techniques section on page 109 to make the hatch opening. Cover the stay with interfacing or felt, and stitch it around the hatch opening, in the same way as for the slots. Place it on the right side of the base, so that it will be inside the money box.

7 Stand the bird house on the base, and stitch the two pieces together as described on page 25.

8 Stitch green felt to the underside of the base to cover all the internal stitching. Cut away the area for the hatch, and stitch the felt to the edge of the opening.

9 ▷ To make the hatch, first cover the tray with felt. Either sandwich it between two pieces and oversew around the edges, or lace a piece of felt to one side and sew or stick felt to the other. Fold the tape in half and stitch it between the layers of felt at the shorter side so that the hatch may be easily opened.

10 ◁ Cover the sides of the tray with felt as shown in the diagram. Stitch them around three sides of the tray leaving one side open to stitch to the base.

11 ▷ Stitch the tray to the hatch opening making sure your stitches are closely worked and secure as this is a moving part, and frequent use will strain the stitches.

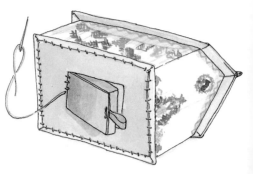

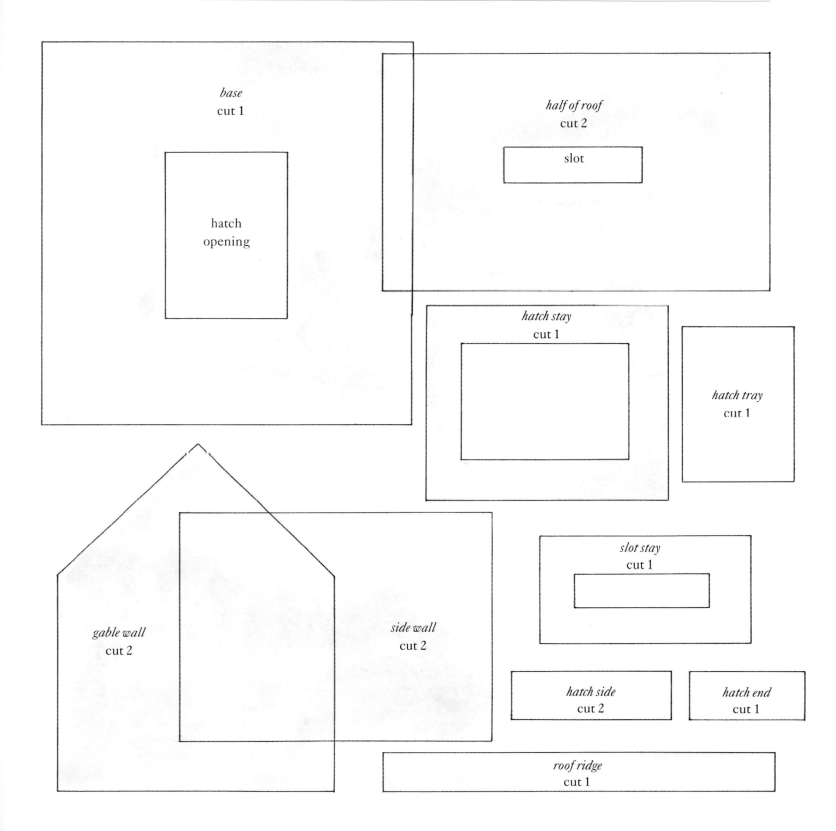

base
cut 1

hatch
opening

half of roof
cut 2

slot

hatch stay
cut 1

hatch tray
cut 1

slot stay
cut 1

gable wall
cut 2

side wall
cut 2

hatch side
cut 2

hatch end
cut 1

roof ridge
cut 1

Cartoon Money Box

Do you know someone saving up to get married? This could be the ideal place for such savings, as the characters on the walls of this house show various stages on the path of true love!

Measurements

The finished size of this money box is 16.5cm tall, 9.5cm wide and 7.5cm deep (6½ x 3¾ x 3in).

Materials

Money boxes must be lined to prevent coins catching in the internal threads, so use the sandwich method, on page 26, to mount the embroidery on the plastic pieces.

- *For the walls:* Piece of antique white 18-count Aida measuring 34 x 20cm (13⅜ x 7⅞in)
- Same-sized piece of interfacing
- *For the roof:* Piece of red 18-count Aida measuring 21 x 12.5cm (8¼ x 5in)
- Same-sized piece of interfacing
- *For the base:* Piece of red 18-count Aida measuring 11.5 x 13.5cm (4½ x 5 ⅜in)

There is no embroidery on the base, so you may use any red fabric. The same-sized piece of interfacing is optional for the base.

- *For the base and the hatch:* Black or red felt measuring 12.5cm square (5in square)
- *To open the hatch:* Black tape 4cm (1½in) long, 5mm (¼in) wide
- *For the stays:* Interfacing or felt 12cm square (4¾in square)
- Iron-on interfacing 5.5 x 3.5cm (2¼ x 1⅜in)
- DMC or Anchor stranded embroidery cotton in the colours shown on the charts
- 7-mesh plastic canvas measuring 28 x 24cm (11 x 9½in)
- Tapestry needle size 26
- Sewing needle

- Matching sewing thread
- Embroidery frame if required

To work the embroidery

The characters around the walls have been given names to make it easier to follow the instructions. The grey-haired couple are Harry and Ethel, the young man at the front door is Tim, and the dreamy couple above him are Janet and Keith. Bob is proposing to Zoe with Sally at the window above them, while on the back wall a lovelorn Sebastian serenades an unappreciative Annabelle.

Stitch the walls on the antique white Aida following the chart on pages 66 and 67. Prepare the fabric as described in the techniques section, on page 109, outlining the area to be stitched with basting stitches, and ironing a piece of interfacing into the slot in the back gable window, above Annabelle's head. Leave an adequate margin all around the walls of 2cm (¾in). Mark the centre of the design to begin stitching, but this is an irregular shape so judge the position of the centre by eye.

All the cross stitches and back stitches are worked using one strand of thread only, but the French and bullion knots (see below) use two strands together. Work each stitch shown on the chart over one square of the fabric, and work all the cross stitches before working first the back stitching, then the knots.

Back stitch following the chart for position and embroidery colours.

French knots and bullion knots

Work all the knots using two strands of thread together in the needle. The blue forget-me-nots at the bottom of the walls are worked in French knots using DMC 794/Anchor 175, and the red roses around the French window are worked in French knots using DMC 321/Anchor 47.

Work a French knot at the centre of Sally's daisy using DMC 972/Anchor 298.

Annabelle's window box contains a red flower called "love-lies-bleeding". This is worked in bullion knots using DMC 814/Anchor 45.

Working the roof

The roof is worked entirely in back stitch following the chart on page 67. Stitch it on the red Aida, using DMC 310/Anchor black. The sides are identical, so when one is complete, turn the work around and stitch the same design on the other side of the ridge.

There is no stitching on the base, so wash and dry the roof and walls as described in the techniques section, page 110.

Cut out the pieces of plastic canvas using the templates provided on page 68. Cut two gable walls, one with a slot, two side walls, two roof pieces and one base. Cut the hatch from the base, then, following the templates given for the Bird House Money Box on page 63, trim the edges to form the tray and cut stays for the hatch and slot and three side pieces for the tray.

Assembling the money box

This piece is constructed in the same way as the Bird House Money Box (see pages 58–62), but without the roof ridge, using the sandwich method.

1 Mount the walls on the plastic canvas, making the slot in the upstairs window as shown on pages 109 and 110. Cover the stay and stitch it around the slot before stitching the side seam in the walls.

2 Mount the roof on the plastic canvas (using the lacing or sandwich method) and stitch it to the walls as described on page 13.

3 Make the base using red fabric. Lay the plastic base on the fabric and mark the position of the hatch. Iron a piece of interfacing to the space for the hatch. Mount the fabric on the plastic canvas base, following the instructions given in the techniques section on page 109 to make the opening for the hatch. Cover the stay with fabric and stitch it around the hatch opening on the right side of the base, not on the underside.

4 Stitch the cartoon house to the base as described on page 25.

5 Follow steps 8 to 11, on page 62 to make the tray for the hatch and to complete the money box, using black or red felt for the tray and to cover the underside of the base.

walls

overlap design from this point ▷

	DMC	Anchor		DMC	Anchor		DMC	Anchor		DMC	Anchor		DMC	Anchor
	415	398		699	923		758	882		369	1043		938	380
	414	400		666	9046		754	1012		783	307		814	45
	413	236		310	black		352	9		798	137		341	117
	blanc	white		801	359		553	99		210	108		890	1044

ridge of roof

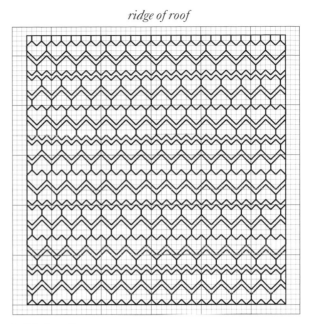

half of roof

◁ overlap design from this point

DMC	Anchor		DMC	Anchor
702	226		904	258
794	175		321	47
972	298			
899	66			

Back stitch			French/Bullion knots	
DMC	Anchor		DMC	Anchor
310	black		814	45
414	400		794	175
413	236		972	298
553	99		321	47
666	9046			
3778	1013			
801	359			
904	258			
938	380			
341	117			
972	298			
783	307			
blanc	white			
814	45			

**Templates for
Cartoon Money Box**

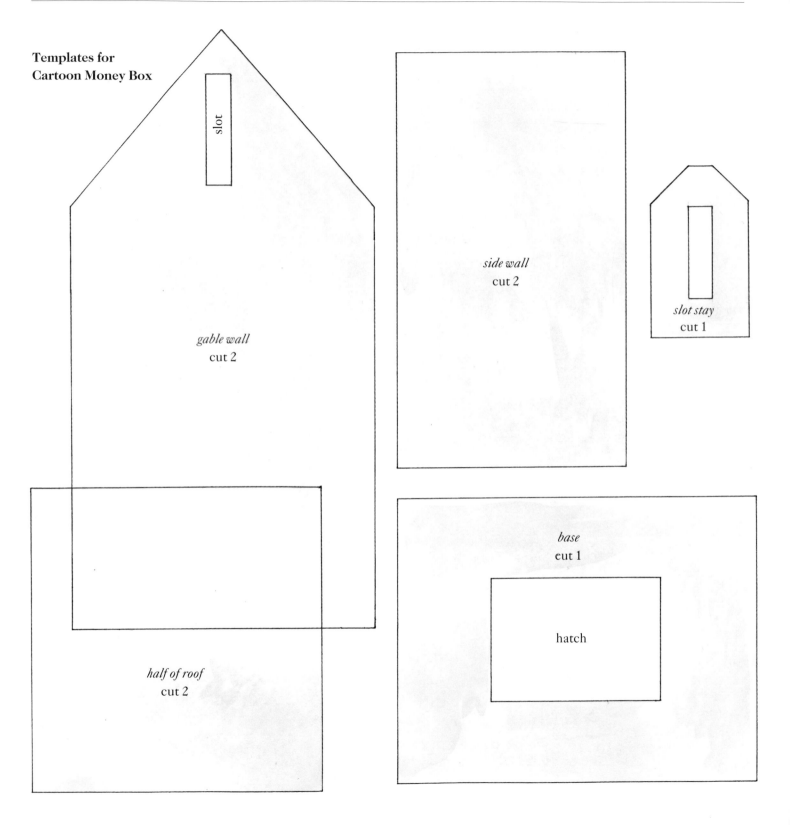

slot

gable wall
cut 2

half of roof
cut 2

side wall
cut 2

slot stay
cut 1

base
cut 1

hatch

Time To Sew Clock

"To everything there is a season, and a time to every purpose under the heaven…a time to rend and a time to sew". Do you know this quote? It can be very comforting in difficult times. This clock shows someone finding time to sew and enjoy the world around them.

Measurements

The finished size of the clock is 14.5cm tall, 9.8cm wide and 5.3cm deep (5¾ x 3⅞ x 2⅛in).

Materials

The main body of the clock is lined to prevent stitches catching in the mechanism, using the sandwich method described on page 26. The base does not need lining.

- *For the clock face:* Piece of antique white 18-count Aida measuring 12.5 x 17.5cm (5 x 7in)
- *For the clock sides:* Piece of antique white 18-count Aida measuring 8 x 36cm (3¼ x 14¼in)
- *For the back, door and base:* Piece of black 28-count Jobelan evenweave measuring 32 x 20cm (12¾ x 8in). There is no embroidery on these pieces, so you may use any suitable black fabric.
- *For the door and base:* Black felt measuring 16 x 9.5cm (6⅜ x 3¾in)
- *For lining the face, back and sides:* Sew-in interfacing measuring 22 x 36cm (8¾ x 14¼in)
- *To open the door:* Black tape 4cm (1½in) long, 5mm (¼in) wide
- Piece of iron-on interfacing 6 x 5cm (2⅜ x 2in)
- *To decorate the clock front:* 65cm (25½in) of black russia braid, approximately 3mm (⅛in) wide
- DMC or Anchor stranded embroidery cotton in the colours shown on the charts
- 7-mesh plastic canvas measuring 18.5 x 27.5cm (7¼ x 10⅞in)

- Clock movement with short spindle, length 10.8mm (⅜in)
- Pair of gold or black clock hands, no longer than 25mm (1in)
- Clock battery suitable for the movement
- Tapestry needle size 26
- Sewing needle
- Matching sewing thread
- Embroidery frame if required

To work the embroidery

Prepare the fabric as described in the techniques section on page 109, marking the areas to be stitched with basting stitches, and leaving margins of 2cm (¾in) around these areas. The sides of the clock are worked in a long piece, with one end appearing upside down when worked. Follow the chart on page 72 and stitch this on the long narrow piece of antique white Aida, turning the fabric round once you have stitched up to the centre line on the chart.

The clock face is worked on the remaining piece of antique white Aida following the chart on page 72. Mark the area where the clock spindle will come through the fabric with basting stitches and iron interfacing to this area.

Much of this design is worked in half cross stitch, so mount it on a frame if possible, to prevent it distorting.

Begin stitching at the centre of each piece and work each stitch over one square of the fabric. Use one strand of thread throughout except for the numbers and French knots on the clock face which are worked using two strands.

Note that the chart for the clock face shows both fractional and half cross stitches as triangles. The half cross stitches form the sky, the meadows, the roadway and the garden lawn. The fractional stitches are used to form the shape of the girl, her clothing, her sewing, the bench she sits on and the spire of the church.

Work all the cross stitches and half cross stitches before the back stitches and French knots.

Back stitch the clock face and sides following the chart for position and embroidery colours.

Wash and dry the face and sides as described in the techniques section on page 110. Cut out the plastic canvas pieces using the templates provided on page 73. Cut a clock face and back, two main side pieces, three side/top pieces and two insert side pieces for the main body. Cut out the area on the clock face for the movement, and the opening for the door on the back. Trim the sides of this piece to make the door. Cut three pieces to form the door sides, the top and bottom of the base, and four base edge pieces.

Assembling the clock

1 ▷ Mount the face and sides on the plastic canvas pieces using the sandwich method, following the diagram for the position of the small side pieces.

Follow the instructions given in the techniques section on page 109 to make the opening for the movement in the clock face.

2 ▷ Ladder stitch the side pieces to the edge of the face and cover this seam with russia braid, turning the ends underneath.

3 Push the spindle of the movement through the opening in the clock face and secure it following the manufacturer's instructions. The movement should be supplied with the necessary washers and nuts and the instructions will explain how to use them. Add the clock hands to the spindle, positioning them at twelve o'clock, and hold them in place with the retaining nut. Put the battery in the movement to check that it is working, and adjust the hands to the right time using the wheel on the movement. The door in the back will let you change the battery or adjust the hands once the clock is in use.

4 Mount the back using the sandwich method, making the opening for the door by following the instructions given in the techniques section on page 109.

5 ▷ Lace black fabric to one side of the door and sew or stick black felt to the other side. Fold the black tape in half and sew it to one edge of the door between the fabrics to act as a handle.

6 ▷ Cover the sides of the door with black felt as described for the tray sides on page 62, step 10, and stitch them around three sides of the door, leaving the sides opposite the handle free. Stitch this edge to the door opening, making it left or right-handed, with the black fabric-covered side of the door on the outside.

7 ▷ Ladder stitch the back to the sides of the clock, being careful not to crush the hands.

8 For the base, cover the top and sides with black fabric, and the bottom with black felt using the lacing method. Join the ends of the sides together and stitch them to the top. Cover the seam with russia braid.

9 ◁ Stand the main body of the clock on the base, and ladder stitch the two together making sure the edges of the base are equal around the clock. Use the same method as for stitching a cottage to a base described on page 25.

10 Fit the felt-covered base bottom inside the edges of the base and stitch it into position.

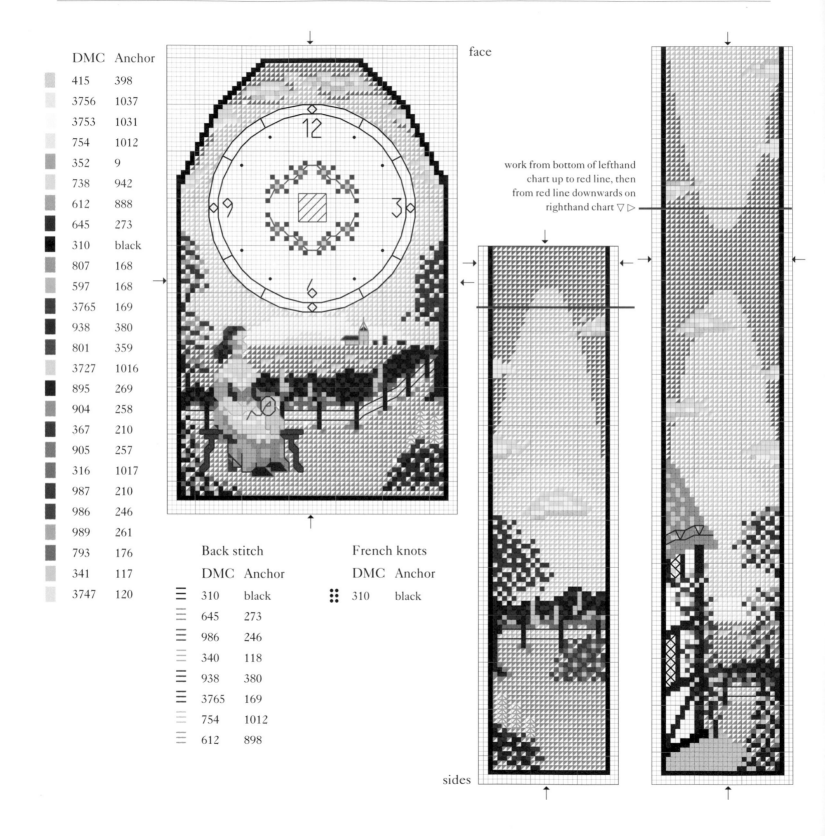

DMC	Anchor
415	398
3756	1037
3753	1031
754	1012
352	9
738	942
612	888
645	273
310	black
807	168
597	168
3765	169
938	380
801	359
3727	1016
895	269
904	258
367	210
905	257
316	1017
987	210
986	246
989	261
793	176
341	117
3747	120

face

work from bottom of lefthand
chart up to red line, then
from red line downwards on
righthand chart ▽ ▷

Back stitch

DMC	Anchor
310	black
645	273
986	246
340	118
938	380
3765	169
754	1012
612	898

French knots

DMC	Anchor
310	black

sides

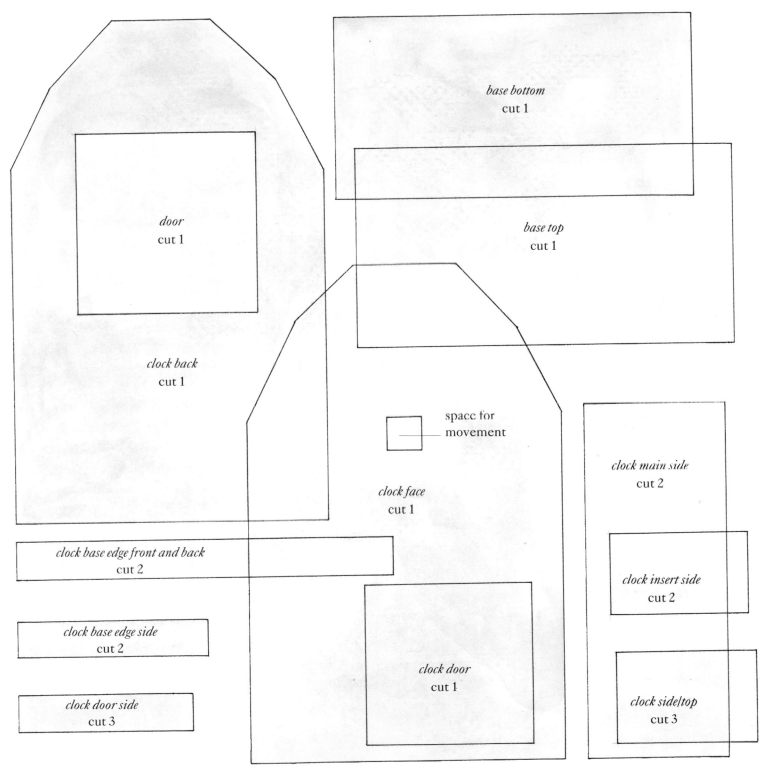

door
cut 1

base bottom
cut 1

base top
cut 1

clock back
cut 1

space for
movement

clock main side
cut 2

clock face
cut 1

clock base edge front and back
cut 2

clock insert side
cut 2

clock base edge side
cut 2

clock door side
cut 3

clock door
cut 1

clock side/top
cut 3

Blue and Silver Jewellery Box

This box is designed for favourite pieces of jewellery. There are several steps to assembling this piece so it is not a simple project, and completing it will give you a real sense of achievement.

Measurements

The finished size of the jewellery box is 6cm high, 11cm wide and 8cm deep (2⅜ x 4⅜ x 3⅛in).

Materials

- *For the lid, sides and drawer front*: Piece of white 18-count Aida measuring 60 x 13cm (23⅝ x 5⅛in)
- *For the base, drawer, tray and lid lining:* Piece of medium blue 28-count Jobelan evenweave measuring 36 x 26cm (14¼ x 10¼in). There is no embroidery on the blue fabric, so you may use any suitable piece of material.
- *For the lid*: Wadding measuring 11 x 8cm (4⅜ x 3⅛in)
- *For the sides, drawer and drawer casing*: Interfacing measuring 38 x 24cm (15 x 9½in)
- *To open the drawer:* White ribbon 4cm (1½in) long, 5mm (¼in) wide
- Iron-on interfacing 4⁵cm x 2⁵cm (1¾ x 1in)
- DMC or Anchor stranded embroidery cotton in the colours shown on the charts
- DMC stranded metallic silver thread
- 7-mesh plastic canvas measuring 22 x 34cm (8¾ x 13½in)
- Tapestry needle size 26
- Sewing needle
- White and blue sewing thread
- Embroidery frame if required

To work the embroidery

Prepare the fabric as described in the techniques section, on page 109, marking the areas to be stitched on the Aida with basting stitches. The lid, lid rim, drawer front and sides are all worked on the white Aida, so place them as shown in the diagram below, leaving a margin of 2cm (¾in) around each piece on all sides. Repeat the pattern for the rim of the lid once to give the required length. It should be the same length as the sides.

Mark the area of the drawer opening and iron interfacing into this space. You could omit the drawer for a simpler design, in which case, just stitch the design for the drawer front into this space. Following the chart on pages 76 and 77, start stitching at the centre, judged by eye, and work each stitch over one square of the fabric. Use one strand of the stranded embroidery thread at a time, but two strands of the metallic thread together. Work all the cross stitches before beginning the French knots and back stitches. Work the back stitch following the chart for position and embroidery colours.

The French knots are worked on the lid and on the oval panels on the chamfered corners of the sides. Keep these knots small by using one strand of thread at a time, and winding it only once or twice around the needle.

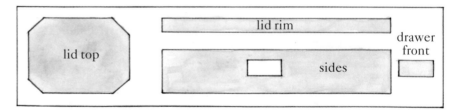

When the embroidery is complete cut out the plastic canvas pieces using the templates provided on page 78.

- *For the lid*: one lid top, back and front of lid rim, two sides of lid rim and four corners of lid rim
- *For the tray*: one tray, back and front of tray edge, two sides of tray edge and four corners of tray edge
- *For the sides*: one back, one front with opening for drawer cut out, two sides and four corners
- *For the drawer*: one drawer front, one drawer back, one drawer base and two drawer sides
- *For the drawer casing*: a top and bottom and two sides
- One base piece

If you want to make a simple box with no drawer, do not cut out the drawer, drawer casing, and tray, but make an inner edge for the lid to fit on. Using the tray edge templates as a guide for the width of the pieces, cut inner sides to extend a little way above the top edge of the sides. When the base and sides have been assembled, cover those inner sides with blue fabric and stand them inside the box. Cover the inside of the base with blue fabric.

To assemble the jewellery box

1 ▽ Begin with the lid. Trim the wadding to the shape of the lid top and oversew it to the plastic with white sewing thread. Work all around the edge of the lid top as shown in the diagram. Lace the embroidered top to the wadding covered plastic top, with the wadding next to the wrong side of the embroidery. Cover the underside of the lid with blue fabric.

2 ▽ Lay the plastic rim pieces on the wrong side of the embroidered rim in the following order, from the left: back-corner-side-corner-front-corner-side-corner. Fix them in one long strip with sticky tape. Lace the embroidered rim to the plastic pieces using white sewing thread. Turn the ends in and stitch down neatly.

3 ▽ Cut a piece of blue fabric the length of the rim by the width plus 1cm (⅜in). Press a seam allowance of 5mm (³⁄₁₆in) to the wrong side of the fabric along each long edge. With blue sewing thread, stitch this piece to the inside of the rim, turning in the raw ends. Stitch the ends together and ladder stitch it to the edge of the lid top, placing the seam at the left back corner. Use matching blue sewing thread and draw the edges together carefully to match the blue picot design on the top and rim.

lid top

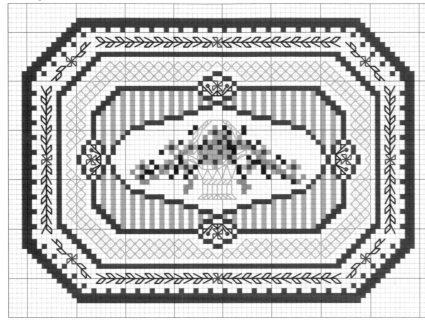

4 If you are going to make the drawer, mount the box sides using the sandwich method (see page 26). Make sure that you insert the plastic pieces in the right order (see instructions for rim in step 2). To make the opening for the drawer in the fabric, follow the instructions given in the techniques section on page 109 .

5 ▷ Make the drawer casing by covering the pieces of plastic canvas with interfacing. Hold them together with sticky tape, and sandwich them between layers of interfacing, sewing around the edges with white sewing thread. Fold them around to form the casing and stitch the seam between the side and top.

DMC	Anchor	Back stitch		French knots	
		DMC	Anchor	DMC	Anchor
798	137			3731	77
986	246	silver	silver		
3731	77	986	246		
989	261	3731	77		
794	175				
3354	74				

drawer front

repeated section

lid rim

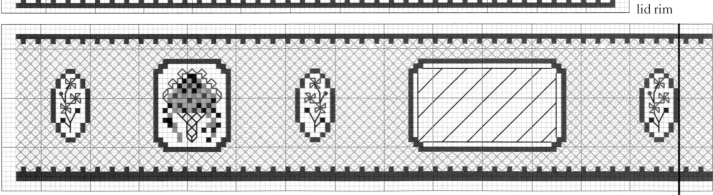

sides

overlap design from this point ▷

6▽ Place one end of the casing on the wrong side of the drawer opening and stitch it in position. Bend the sides around so that the back is opposite the front and sew the other end of the casing to the back. Ladder stitch the side ends together.

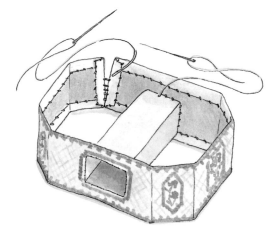

7 Cut a piece of blue fabric for the base using the template, and adding 2cm (¾in) to all sides, then lace it to the plastic canvas base. Stand the sides on the base with the fabric covered side outwards and ladder stitch the two pieces together.

8 Lace blue fabric to the plastic canvas tray as for the base. Lay the pieces of the tray edge in a long line as for the lid rim and hold them together with sticky tape. Cut a piece of blue fabric the length of the tray edge plus 2.5cm (1in) and double the width plus 1.5cm (⅝in). Using an iron, press a seam allowance along each long edge as for the lid rim, then fold the fabric in half along the length, wrong sides together, and press again.

9 ▷ Put the tray edge pieces inside the fabric and oversew the edges together using blue sewing thread. Turn in the ends and stitch them neatly together. Sew the edges around the blue tray, and stand it inside the jewellery box. It should rest on the drawer casing with the edges standing above the sides so that the lid will fit over them. Stitch the tray to the sides.

10▷ Make the drawer. Lace the embroidered drawer front to the plastic canvas drawer front, and cover the back with interfacing. Lace blue fabric to the drawer bottom, and cover the underside with interfacing. Cover the sides and back of the draw with blue fabric as for the tray edge. Stitch the sides and back around the edge of the base. Fold the white ribbon in half and attach it to the drawer and stitch the drawer front in position.

◁ overlap design from this point

Templates for Blue and Silver Jewellery Box

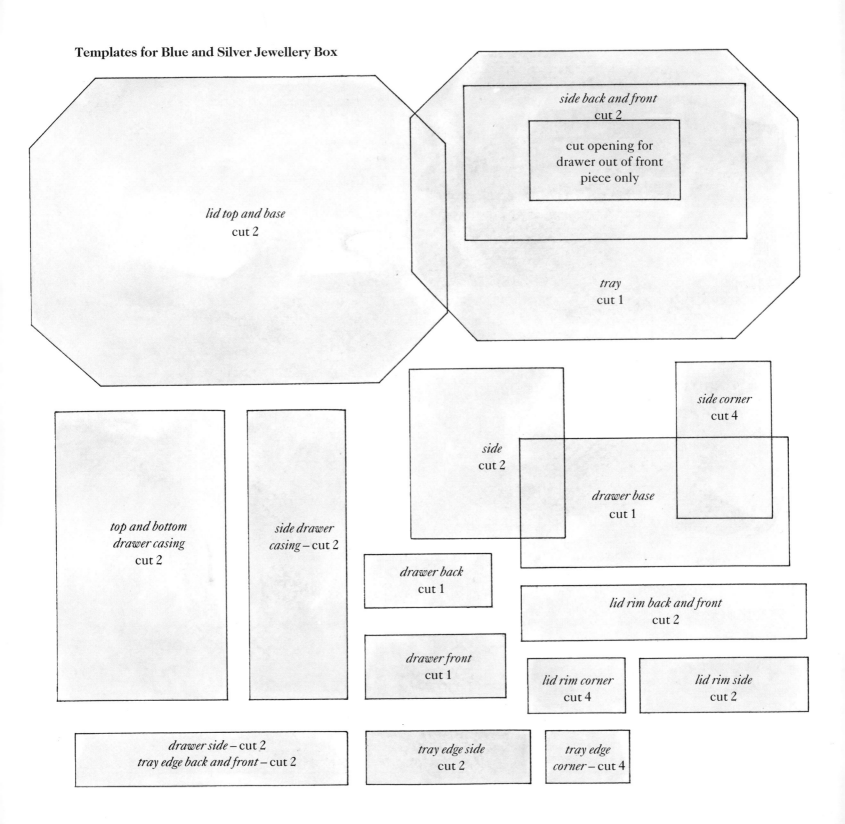

lid top and base
cut 2

side back and front
cut 2

cut opening for
drawer out of front
piece only

tray
cut 1

side corner
cut 4

side
cut 2

drawer base
cut 1

*top and bottom
drawer casing*
cut 2

*side drawer
casing* – cut 2

drawer back
cut 1

lid rim back and front
cut 2

drawer front
cut 1

lid rim corner
cut 4

lid rim side
cut 2

drawer side – cut 2
tray edge back and front – cut 2

tray edge side
cut 2

*tray edge
corner* – cut 4

Silhouette Trinket Box

Make this heart-shaped box as a gift for someone special, or keep it on your own dressing table to store a favourite locket or pair of earrings.

Measurements

The finished size of the silhouette box is 3.5cm high, 7.5cm wide and 7cm deep (1⅜ x 3 x 2⅜in).

Materials

- *For the lid and sides*: Piece of white 20-count Aida measuring 27 x 14cm (10⅝ x 5½in)

- *For the base, sides and lid*: Piece of black 28-count Jobelan evenweave measuring 25 x19cm (9⅞ x 7½in). There is no embroidery on the black fabric, so you may use any suitable material.

- *For the lid*: Wadding measuring 8cm square (3⅛in square)

- *For the base*: Black felt measuring 8cm square (3⅛in square)

- 50cm (20in) narrow black braid, e.g. russia braid

- DMC or Anchor stranded embroidery cotton in the colours shown on the charts

- Madeira metallic thread no.40, colour gold-7

- Two ready-made heart-shaped pieces of plastic canvas, size 7.5cm (3in)

- 7-mesh plastic canvas measuring 11cm square (4⅜in square)

- Tapestry needle size 26

- Sewing needle

- White and black sewing thread

- Embroidery frame if required

To work the embroidery

Prepare the fabric as described in the techniques section on page 109, marking the areas to be stitched on the white Aida with basting stitches. Work one top and two identical sides. Position

DMC	Anchor
415	398
310	black

Back stitch

DMC	Anchor
Madeira gold	
000	black

French knots

Madeira gold

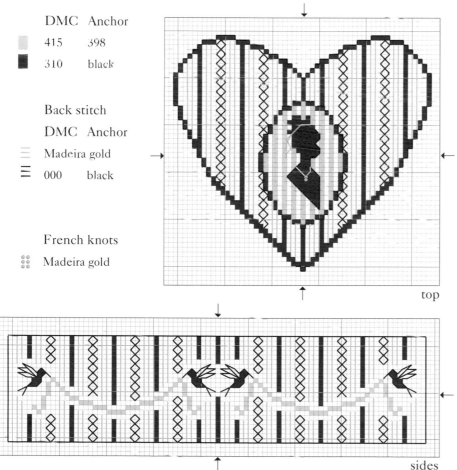

top

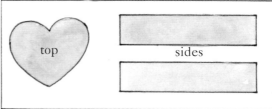

top   sides

sides

the top and sides of the box as shown in the diagram on page 79. Make sure you leave sufficient margin around the pieces on all sides.

Mark the centre of each piece and begin stitching at this point, following the charts on page 79. Use one strand of thread at a time except for the gold metallic thread. This is not divisible, so cut two lengths of thread and use them together. Work each stitch over one square of the fabric and complete all the cross stitches before beginning the back stitch.

Back stitch following the charts for position and embroidery colours.

If possible, avoid washing these pieces when you have completed the stitching.

Cut two box sides, and two base rim pieces from the plastic canvas using the templates provided on page 81.

Assembling the trinket box

1 The plastic canvas hearts have small hooks at the top. Trim these away on both hearts, and trim away the edging – the 3mm (⅛in) wide border around the heart – on one of them. This heart will be used for the top, so lay the other aside to use for the base.

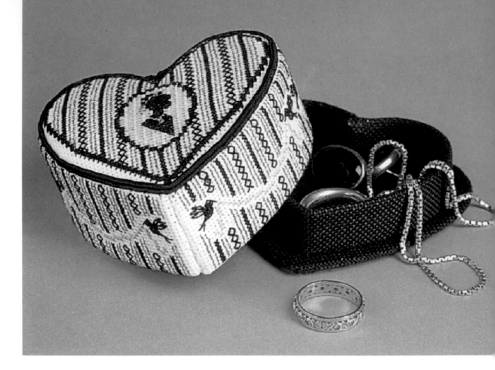

2 ▷ Cover the top plastic heart with wadding, following the instructions given for the jewellery box lid on page 75, step 1. Cut the embroidered top from the fabric and trim it to shape, leaving a 2cm (¾in) margin all around the embroidery. Run gathering threads around the margin, starting at the middle, working down the side, and ending at the lower point of the heart.

3 ▷ Lay the wadding-covered plastic heart on the wrong side of the embroidery, and gently pull up the gathering threads, so that the fabric margin curls over the plastic. Snip carefully between the two halves of the heart at the top to allow the fabric to lie flat, but do not make the cut more than half the width of the turning. When the fabric is stretched over the plastic without distorting it, fasten off the gathering threads, and lace the fabric to the heart to give a smooth surface to the box. Sew black fabric to the underside of the heart.

4 Cut the embroidered sides from the fabric, leaving a margin around each piece on all sides, and lace them to the plastic canvas sides. Stitch two short ends together to form one long strip.

5 Cut black fabric to line the sides as described in step 3 on page 75, lining the rim of the jewellery box lid, and press in seam allowances with an iron. Stitch this piece to the sides as lining, but pull gently on the fabric as you go so that the sides curve in slightly. This will prevent the lining sagging when the sides are sewn in position as it is on an inside curve. Turn in the ends and sew them neatly down.

6 ◁ Ladder stitch the sides to the top, beginning at the centre of the heart, working down to the lower point and up the remaining side to the centre. Stitch the remaining ends of the sides together. Stitch braid over this seam to hide the stitches.

7 ▽ For the base, cover the remaining heart in black fabric, following the method described in step 2 using gathering threads. Cover the rim of the base in black fabric, following the method described on page 77, steps 8 and 9 to cover the edges of the jewellery box tray. Sew the ends of the rim together, and bend them into a heart shape. Stand them on the base with an equal margin around them, and ladder stitch the two pieces together in the same way as for stitching a cottage to a base as described on page 25.

Sew or stick felt to the underside of the base to cover all the internal stitching.

The top of the silhouette box will fit over the rim, which will hold it in position.

base rim
cut 2

box side
cut 2

Green Trinket Box

This box is slightly smaller than the Silhouette Trinket Box and is stitched in colours to match the green vase on the following pages. You could stitch this piece in any choice of colours to make it a more personal gift.

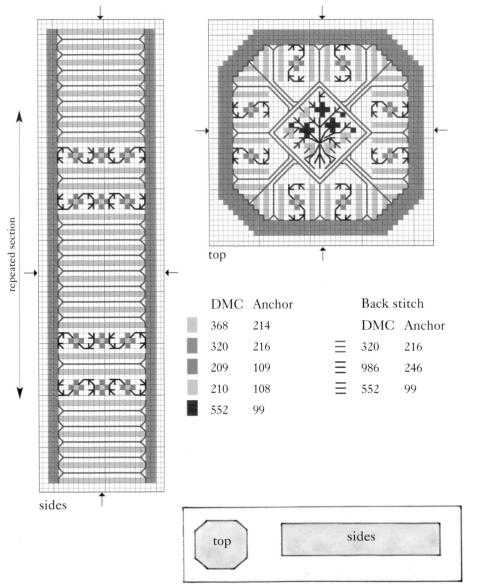

repeated section

top

sides

DMC	Anchor		Back stitch	
			DMC	Anchor
368	214			
320	216		320	216
209	109		986	246
210	108		552	99
552	99			

top   sides

Measurements

The finished size of the silhouette box is 3cm high, 5.5cm wide and 5.5cm deep (1³⁄₁₆ x 2⅛ x 2⅛in).

Materials

- *For the lid and sides:* Piece of white 20-count Aida measuring 30.5 x 9cm (12 x 3½in)
- *For the base, lid and sides:* Piece of light green 28-count Jobelan evenweave measuring 22 x 15cm (8¾ x 6in). There is no embroidery on the green fabric, so you may use any suitable piece of material.
- *For the lid*: Wadding measuring 5cm square (2in square)
- *For the base*: Green felt measuring 6cm square (2⅜in square)
- DMC or Anchor stranded embroidery cotton in the colours shown on the charts
- 7-mesh plastic canvas measuring 13.5 x 11.5cm (5¼ x 4½in)
- Tapestry needle size 26
- Sewing needle
- White and green sewing thread
- Embroidery frame if required

To work the embroidery

Mark the areas to be stitched on the white Aida fabric with basting stitches, following the instructions in the techniques section on page 109. Place the top and sides as shown in the diagram.

Mark the centre of each piece and begin to stitch at this point, following the charts on page 82. Use one strand of thread, and work each cross stitch shown on the chart over one square of the fabric. Work all the cross stitches before beginning the back stitch. The chart for the sides shows only part of the length, repeat the area shown for the full length of the sides.

Back stitch following the chart for position and embroidery colours.

Wash and dry the pieces as described in the techniques section on page 110.

Cut out the plastic canvas pieces using the templates provided on page 84. Cut out one top, one base, four sides and four corners for the sides, and four side rims and four corner rims for the edge of the base.

Assembling the trinket box

1 This piece is made in the same way as the trinket box on pages 79–81. First cover the top with wadding, oversewing it down around the edge (see the jewellery box on page 75).

2 Lace the embroidered top to the wadding-covered top, stretching it over the wadding without distorting the shape. Cover the underside of the top with light green fabric.

3 Lay the side pieces in a line alternating the corners and sides. Hold them together with sticky tape, and lace the embroidered sides to the plastic sides keeping the flower motifs against the side pieces and the green stripes against the corner pieces. Turn in the ends and stitch down neatly.

4 Cut a piece of green fabric to line the sides as described in step 3 of the instructions for the jewellery box on page 75. Press in a seam allowance and stitch it to the sides, pulling gently on the fabric as you do so to make the sides curve in a little. Turn in the ends of the lining, sew them neatly in position and stitch the ends of the sides together.

5 Ladder stitch the sides to the top, setting the side seam at the top left corner and being careful to match the position of the flowers on the sides with those on the top. Pull gently on the thread to bring the green edges together without leaving a gap of white fabric between the top and sides, but if necessary this seam can be covered with a length of suitable braid.

6 Cover the base with green fabric, using the lacing method. Make the rim for the base as described in step 8 on page 77 (making the edge of the jewellery box tray), alternating corners and sides of the rim. Ladder stitch the rim to the base, as described on page 25.

7 Sew or stick green felt to the underside of the base to cover the internal stitching. The top of the box should fit over the rim of the base, which will hold it in position.

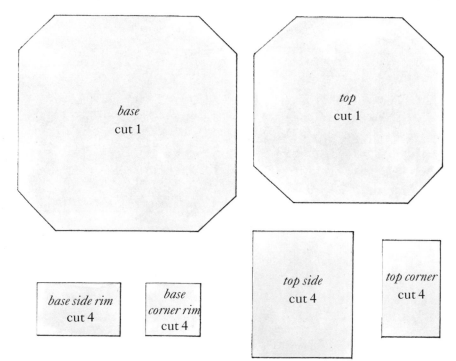

base
cut 1

top
cut 1

base side rim
cut 4

base corner rim
cut 4

top side
cut 4

top corner
cut 4

Flower Vase

This vase has a simple shape, and you will not find it difficult to make. It will hold silk or paper flowers, or even fresh flowers if you place a small test tube of water inside it.

Measurements

The finished size of the vase is 10cm high, 4.3cm wide and 4.3cm deep (4 x 11¾ x 1¾in)

Materials – For the blue colourway

- *For the body of the vase*: Piece of white 20-count Aida measuring 23 x 17cm (9 x 6⅜in)
- *To line the vase*: Piece of sew-in interfacing measuring 12 x 10cm (4¾ x 4in)
- *For the base*: Royal blue or white felt measuring 4.5cm (1¾in) square
- *For the top*: White felt measuring 4.5cm (1¾in) square
- Iron-on interfacing 2.5cm (1in) square
- DMC or Anchor stranded embroidery cotton in the colours shown on the charts
- 7-mesh plastic canvas measuring 15 x 10cm (6 x 4in)
- Tapestry needle size 26 or 28
- Sewing needle
- Matching sewing thread
- Embroidery frame if required

N.B. For the green colourway, substitute green felt for blue and use the stranded embroidery cotton in the colours shown in brackets on the chart key, except where noted.

To work the embroidery

First prepare the Aida fabric as explained in the section on techniques on page 109 by marking the outline of the pieces and the centre of each piece with basting stitches. Make sure there is a margin of 2cm (¾in) around the pieces on all sides. The top of the vase will have a square hole cut from the centre. Follow the instructions in the techniques section on page 109 for preparing an opening and iron interfacing into the area to be cut out before stitching.

Position the pieces on the fabric as shown in the diagram below and begin your stitching at the centre of each piece.

The vase is worked using one strand of embroidery thread, and each cross stitch is worked over one square of the fabric. The chart on page 87 shows two sides of the vase. Repeat the area shown to give all four sides. Follow the charts, and work all the cross stitches before the back stitching. Follow the chart for the colours and position of the back stitches.

Once the stitching of the vase pieces has been completed, wash and dry the fabric following the instructions given in the techniques section on page 110. The vase will then be ready to assemble.

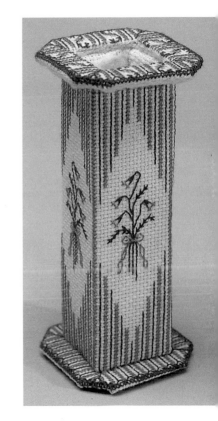

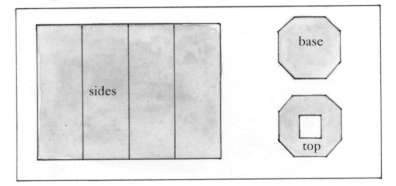

3 Before bending the walls around to form a cylinder, line them with sew-in interfacing, or any lining fabric. This will prevent the stems of the flowers from catching in the lacing threads.

4 Bend the sides round to form a three-dimensional shape, and ladder stitch the seam between the sides of the vase.

5 Mount the base and top of the vase, lacing them to the plastic as before. Follow the instructions in the techniques section on page 109 to make the opening in the top and cover the underside with white felt.

6 ▷ Stitch the body of the vase to the base. Stand it in position and bring your needle up through the base. Take a small stitch in the bottom edge of the vase and pass the needle back down through the base, pushing it through the holes in the plastic canvas. Work all around the sides of the vase, making sure it is securely attached to the base, and that it will stand upright when set on a hard surface.

7 ▷ Ladder stitch the top of the vase to the top edge of the walls.

8 Sew or stick blue or white felt to the underside of the base to cover the internal stitching, and fill your vase with flowers.

Assembling the vase

1 Cut four side pieces, a top and a base from the plastic canvas using templates provided on page 87. The top piece has a square cut out from the centre for the vase opening.

2 Cut the walls of the vase from the fabric, making sure there is a 2cm (¾in) margin around them on all sides, and lace them to the plastic walls following the instructions on page 12.

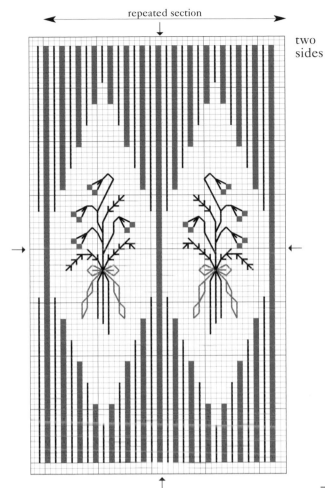

repeated section

two sides

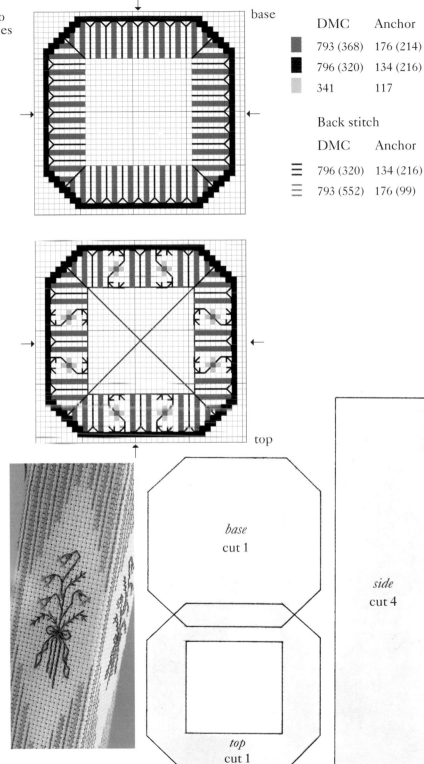

base

DMC	Anchor
793 (368)	176 (214)
796 (320)	134 (216)
341	117

Back stitch

DMC	Anchor
796 (320)	134 (216)
793 (552)	176 (99)

top

Working the green colourway

To make the vase in the green colourway you will need the materials listed on page 85, with the alternative colours mentioned in the note.

To work the embroidery

Work from the same charts but with the following changes: work the flowers on the sides in DMC 209/Anchor 109; the flowers on the top in DMC 209/Anchor 109 with a centre of DMC 368/ Anchor 214; work the flower tendrils and stalks on the top and sides in DMC 986/Anchor 246.

When all the embroidery is complete, follow the instructions given for assembling the vase, remembering to use green felt instead of blue to cover the underside of the base.

base
cut 1

side
cut 4

top
cut 1

Doll's house Furniture

Here are more designs to make practical use of your skills. These pieces will provide attractive and necessary additions to several doll's house rooms: the sitting room, the bedroom, the nursery and the playroom. With the exception of the toy box, each piece has an inner plastic frame for support. The cross-stitched fabric is attached to the frame to represent soft furnishings. These pieces should be suitable for a one-twelfth size doll's house.

Sofa, Chair and Footstool

This comfortable sofa with its matching chair and footstool would grace the sitting room of any self-respecting doll. Alternatively, in pastel colours, they would be perfect for the bedroom.

Measurements

The finished size of the sofa is 9cm tall, 13.5cm wide and 4.5cm deep (3 9/16 x 5 5/16 x 1¾in).

The finished size of the chair is 9cm tall, 7.5cm wide and 4.5cm deep (3 9/16 x 3 x 1¾in).

The finished size of the footstool is 3.5cm tall, 4.5cm wide and 3.5cm deep (1⅜ x 1¾ x 1⅜in).

Materials

For the Sofa

- *To cover the sofa and make two cushions*: Piece of red 28-count Jobelan evenweave measuring 46 x 24cm (18⅛ x 9½in)
- *To make the frame for the arms and back*: Piece of antique sage 18-count Aida measuring 38 x 12cm (15 x 4¾in)
- Piece of wadding measuring 13cm square (5⅛in square)
- *To cover the inner frame*: Piece of sew-in interfacing measuring 30 x 8cm (11¾ x 3⅛in)
- DMC or Anchor stranded embroidery cotton in the colours shown on the charts
- 7-mesh plastic canvas measuring 22.5 x 12.5cm (8⅞ x 4⅞in)

For the Armchair

- *To cover the chair and make one cushion*: Piece of red 28-count Jobelan evenweave measuring 36 x 24cm (14⅛ x 9½in)
- *To make the frame for the arms and back*: Piece of antique sage 18-count Aida measuring 26.5 x 12cm (10½ x 4¾in)
- Piece of wadding measuring 20 x 6cm (7⅞ x 2⅜in)
- *To cover the inner frame*: Piece of sew-in interfacing measuring 18 x 8cm (7⅛ x 3⅛in)
- DMC or Anchor stranded embroidery cotton in the colours shown on the charts
- 7-mesh plastic canvas measuring 20 x 8.5cm (7⅞ x 3⅜in)

For the Footstool

- *To cover the stool*: Piece of red 28-count Jobelan evenweave measuring 34.5 x 7cm (13⅝ x 2¾in)
- *To make the trim*: Piece of antique sage 18-count Aida measuring 20 x 2cm (7⅞ x ¾in)
- Piece of wadding measuring 4 x 3cm (1⅝ x 1¼in)
- *To cover the inner frame*: Piece of sew-in interfacing measuring 13 x 6.5cm (5⅛ x 2⅝in)
- DMC or Anchor stranded embroidery cotton in the colours shown on the charts
- 7-mesh plastic canvas measuring 14 x 4cm (5½ x 1⅝in)

For the Sofa, Chair and Footstool

- Tapestry needle size 26
- Sewing needle
- Matching sewing thread
- Embroidery frame if required

To work the embroidery for the Sofa

Work the frames for the back and arms on the antique sage Aida. Prepare the fabric as described in the techniques section, page 109, marking the separate areas for stitching on the fabric with basting stitches. Mark the whole area for the back and arms as shown in the diagram opposite, making sure there is a suitable margin around

stitching across the width of the fabric with sufficient margin between them. Following the charts on page 92, begin stitching at the centre of each piece, judged by eye, and use two strands of thread for the cross stitches and one strand for the back stitches. Work each stitch over two threads of the fabric and complete all the cross stitches before the back stitching, which is worked using DMC 783/Anchor 307.

When these pieces are finished, you may start to assemble the sofa. The skirt and trim will be worked later. If necessary, wash and dry the embroidery.

Using the templates provided on page 96, cut the pieces for the sofa from the plastic canvas. Cut one back, two arms and one seat for the top, and a back, front and two sides for the base.

each piece. Stitch one of the arms for the right side of the sofa and one as a mirror image for the left side. The remaining Aida fabric will be used to make the trim.

Following the charts on page 92, begin stitching at the centre, judged by eye, and work all the cross stitches first, then the back stitches, using one strand of thread at a time. Work each stitch over one square of the Aida fabric.

The back, arms and seat of the sofa are worked on the red Jobelan evenweave. Mark the areas for

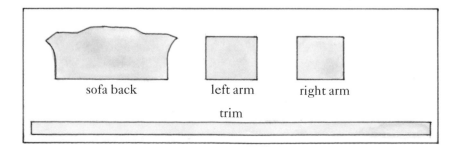

sofa back   left arm   right arm

trim

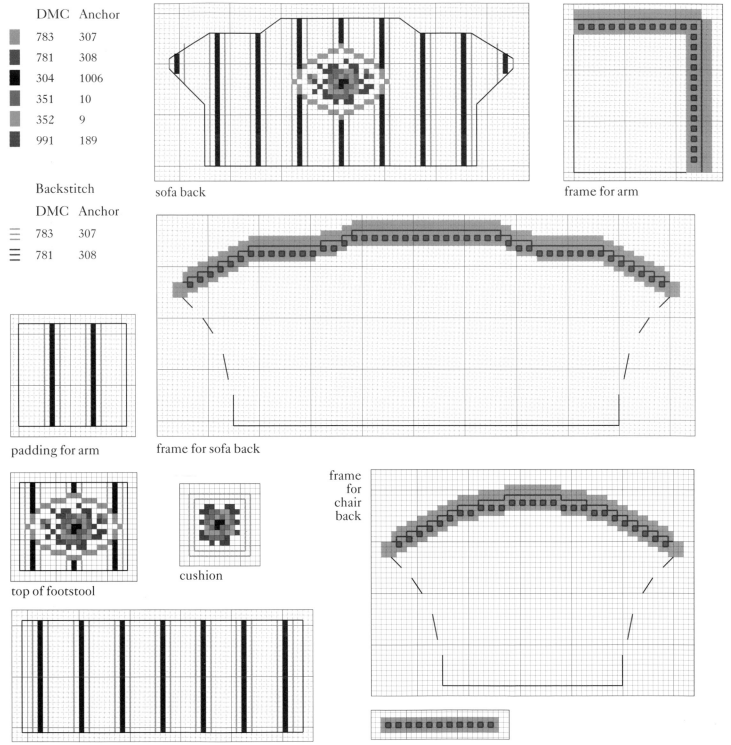

DMC   Anchor
783   307
781   308
304   1006
351   10
352   9
991   189

Backstitch
DMC   Anchor
783   307
781   308

sofa back

frame for arm

padding for arm

frame for sofa back

top of footstool

cushion

frame for chair back

sofa seat

pattern for trim (repeat across width of fabric)

Assembling the Sofa

1 ▷ Mount the cross-stitched frames for the back and arms on the plastic canvas pieces using the lacing method. The cross stitching should be folded along the continuous line of back stitching, so that the stitching for the frame is on the back and front of the plastic.

2 ▷ Using the pattern provided on page 95, cut a piece of wadding for the back. Place it on the wrong side of the red embroidered back and turn the seam allowance over the wadding, holding it in place with a few stitches.

3 ▷ Lay the red back piece on the Aida-covered frame, placing it just below the cross-stitched top with the sides and bottom together. Ladder stitch the top edge just below the cross stitching on the frame and oversew the sides and bottom.

4 Prepare the arms in the same way, mounting the red embroidered pieces on the wadding and sewing them to the frame just inside the cross stitching.

5 Cut a piece of wadding the same size as the plastic seat, and sew it to the plastic as described for the lid of the jewellery box, on page 75, step 1. Lace the red embroidered seat to the wadding covered seat. Make sure the centre of the design is in the centre of the seat to match the sofa back.

6 ◁ Stitch the back, seat and arms together by oversewing the edges.

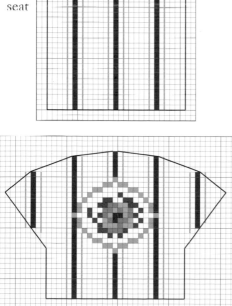

chair
seat

chair back

7 ◁ For the base, lay the plastic pieces in a strip, alternating sides, back and front, and hold them together with sticky tape. Cover these pieces with interfacing, bend into shape, and stitch the seam between the back and side.

8 ▽ Place the sofa top on the frame and stitch the two pieces together.

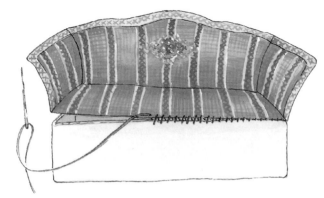

9 ◁ Cut a piece of red fabric 24 x 7cm (9½ x 2¾in) to cover the back. This will be stitched to the back of the frame, stretching from the outside edge of one arm, across the back and along the other arm. Fold in a seam allowance of 5mm (¼in) along the top edge and leave an allowance at the side to be turned in and stitched down later.

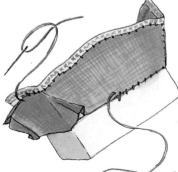

Work along the top of the sofa, stitching the fabric just below the cross stitches on the Aida. It will not lie flat at the corners, so tuck the extra fabric into a pleat and stitch down this edge. Turn in the fabric at the sides and stitch it down. Sew or tack the backing fabric to the bottom edge of the sofa top.

10 ◁ To make the skirt, cut a piece of red fabric 42 x 8cm (16½ x 3⅛in). Bring the long edges together and

iron down the fold at the lower edge. Stitch the striped pattern from the sofa seat on the top layer of the skirt only, down to the fold, working each stitch over two threads. Mark the centre of the long edge, which will match the centre stripe on the seat. Set the red stripe of the pattern in the centre and work lines of back stitch either side of it with DMC 783/Anchor307. Set the stripes five stitches apart, and work three more stripes one side of the centre stripe. At the corner of the sofa there will be an inverted pleat.

Fold the pleat into place, using 2cm (¾in) of fabric, and hold it with basting stitches. Continue with the striped pattern, measuring the skirt against the sofa as a guide. Make another pleat for the back corner and continue to work along the back edge of the skirt until it will reach to the centre of the sofa back. Return to the centre of the skirt and work three repeats of the stripe pattern the other side of the centre stripe, followed by a corner pleat.

11 ▽ Complete this side of the skirt, making another pleat for the remaining corner. Press the pleats with an iron and oversew the top and side edges of the skirt together. Placing the centre stripe of the skirt to match the centre stripe of the seat, sew the skirt around the sofa with the pleats at the corners. At the back, turn one end over and sew it down.

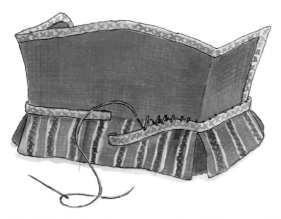

12 △ Work the trim on a length of Aida cut to fit around the sofa. Following the chart on page 92, work the pattern all along the fabric. Turn the raw edges to the back of the stitching and slip stitch together. Sew the trim around the sofa, covering the seam between the top and skirt.

Making a Cushion

To make a Cushion, use any remaining fabric. Following the chart on page 92, use two strands of thread for the cross stitches, and one strand of thread for the back stitches. Cut out the cushion, leaving a seam allowance around the embroidery, and cut another piece of fabric the same size. With right sides facing, stitch around three sides. Turn right side out and stuff with wadding. Turn in the raw edges and sew together.

To make the Chair

Follow the instructions for the Sofa. Work the embroidery as described on pages 90 and 91. Use the templates given for the back, seat and base of the chair, but use the same patterns and templates for the arms of the chair as for the sofa, and follow the assembly instructions on page 93. At steps 9 and 10, measure the chair carefully before cutting the fabric for backing the chair and making the skirt. The piece for the backing should be about 17 x 7cm (6¾ x 2¾in) and the piece for the skirt about 34 x 8cm (13⅜ x 3 ⅛in).

To make the Footstool

The Footstool is made using the same techniques as the Sofa and Chair. Following the chart on page 92, stitch the stool top on the red Jobelan evenweave. Follow the instructions for working the embroidery for the Sofa on pages 90 and 91. Cut out the plastic pieces using the templates given on page 96. Cut a stool top, and a front, back and two sides for the base. Cover the top with wadding and lace the red embroidered top over it as described for the sofa seat, page 93, step 5.

Make the inner frame by covering the base pieces with interfacing as described for the sofa, page 94, step 7, and sew the stool top to the frame.

For the skirt, cut a piece of red fabric 25 x 6.5cm (9⅞ x 2⅝in) and prepare it as for the sofa skirt, page 94, step 10. Embroider the striped pattern on the stool's skirt, and make the inverted pleats at the corners as for the sofa.
▷ Stitch the skirt around the edge of the footstool, and cover the seam with a piece of trim as described in step 12 above.

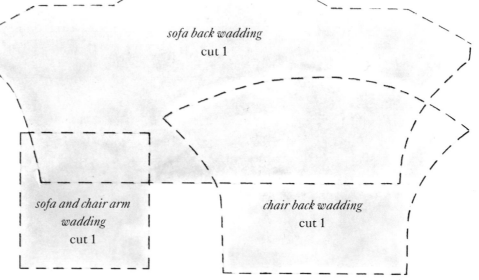

sofa back wadding
cut 1

sofa and chair arm wadding
cut 1

chair back wadding
cut 1

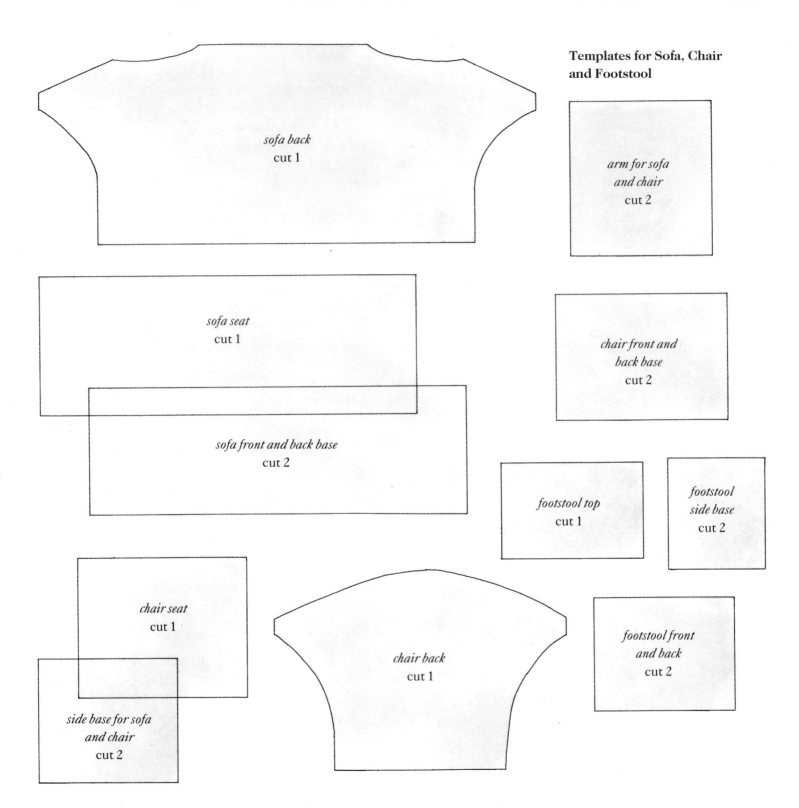

Templates for Sofa, Chair and Footstool

sofa back
cut 1

*arm for sofa
and chair*
cut 2

sofa seat
cut 1

*chair front and
back base*
cut 2

sofa front and back base
cut 2

footstool top
cut 1

*footstool
side base*
cut 2

chair seat
cut 1

chair back
cut 1

*footstool front
and back*
cut 2

*side base for sofa
and chair*
cut 2

Bed, Bed Linen and Dressing Table

This delicate violet and white single bed, made up with a pillow and matching quilt, and the co-ordinating dressing table could be placed in the best spare bedroom.

Measurements

The finished size of the bed is 9cm tall, 8cm wide and 15.7cm long (3½ x 3¼ x 6¼in).

The finished size of the dressing table is 11.5cm tall, 10cm wide and 4.5cm deep (4½ x 4 x 1¾in).

Materials

For the Bed, Quilt and Pillow

- *For the bed, mattress and pillow*: Piece of white 28-count Jobelan evenweave measuring 46 x 21cm (18⅛ x 8¼in)
- *For the bedhead*: Piece of white 18-count Aida measuring 11.5 x 14cm (4⅝ x 5½in)
- *For the mattress, quilt and pillow*: Piece of 2.5cm (1in) thick wadding measuring 25 x 19cm (9⅞ x 7½in)
- *For the inner frame*: Piece of white sew-in interfacing measuring 19 x 30cm (7½ x 11⅞in)
- *For the quilt*: Two pieces of 28-count Jobelan evenweave measuring 17 x 19cm (6¾ x 7½in), one violet and one white
- DMC or Anchor stranded embroidery cotton in the colours shown on the charts
- 7-mesh plastic canvas measuring 22 x 15cm (8¾ x 6in)

For the Dressing Table

- *For the skirt*: Piece of white 28-count Jobelan evenweave measuring 14 x 25cm (5½ x 9⅞in)
- *For the table top and mirror frame*: Piece of white 18-count Aida measuring 23 x 13.5cm (9 x 5⅜in)
- *For the inner frame*: Piece of sew-in interfacing measuring 24cm square (9½in square)
- *For the mirror frame*: Piece of iron-on interfacing measuring 3 x 3.5cm (1¼ x 1⅜in)
- DMC or Anchor stranded embroidery cotton in the colours shown on the charts
- 7-mesh plastic canvas measuring 23 x 13cm (9⅛ x 5⅛in)
- Mirror card measuring 5.5 x 4.5cm (2¼ x 1¾in)
- 50 cm (19¾in) of narrow white braid

For all pieces

- Tapestry needle size 26
- Sewing needle
- Matching sewing thread
- Embroidery frame if required

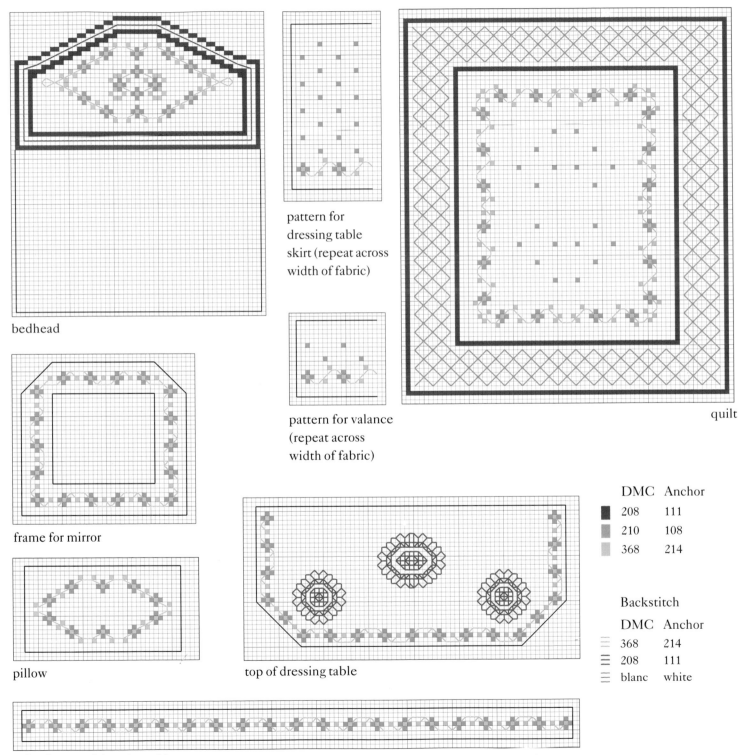

bedhead

pattern for
dressing table
skirt (repeat across
width of fabric)

pattern for valance
(repeat across
width of fabric)

quilt

frame for mirror

pillow

top of dressing table

DMC	Anchor
208	111
210	108
368	214

Backstitch

DMC	Anchor
368	214
208	111
blanc	white

edge for top of dressing table

To work the embroidery for the Bed

Stitch the design for the bedhead on the white Aida. Prepare the fabric as described in the techniques section on page 109. Mark the whole area for the bedhead with basting stitches, although the design is only on the top half, and leave a suitable margin on all sides. Following the chart on page 98, begin to cross stitch at the centre of the design, judged by eye, using one strand of thread throughout and working over one square of the fabric. Many of the back stitches are worked over two squares, so follow the chart to place them correctly.

Wash and dry the fabric if necessary, as described in the techniques section on page 110.

The valance will be stitched at a later stage. Using the templates provided on page 102, cut out the plastic canvas pieces. Cut one bedhead, one base, two long sides and one foot.

Assembling the Bed

1 ▽ First make the inner frame. Lay the bed base on the working surface with the long sides either side of it and the foot at one end. Hold the pieces together with sticky tape and cover them with interfacing by cutting two rectangles measuring 19 x 14.5cm (7½ x 5¾in). Stitch round all four sides to enclose them, then stitch between the pieces to hold them in place. To make the box shape, bring the edges of the sides and foot together. The fabric between them will form a pleat on the wrong side of the base. Stitch the edges together and trim away the spare fabric.

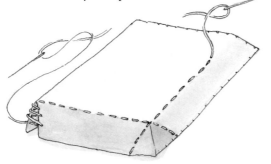

2 ▷ Make the valance in the same way as the sofa skirt. Cut a piece of white Jobelan evenweave 46 x 7cm (18⅛ x 2¾in) and press a fold along the length, as described in step 10, page 94. Following the chart on page 98, stitch the design for the valance on the top layer of fabric only and begin at one side, 1.5cm (⅝in) in from the end to allow for neatening the edge. Work all the cross stitches using two strands of thread. Work the back stitches with one strand of thread only, using DMC 368/Anchor 214. Repeat the design shown on the chart until the valance will cover one side of the bed, and then make an inverted pleat as described in step 10 on page 94. Continue with the cross-stitched design until the foot of the bed is covered and make another pleat. Work the design on the remaining fabric until there is enough to cover the second side. Wash and dry the valance if necessary, pressing the pleats with an iron, and oversew the top and side edges together. Turn in the ends, and sew them to the reverse to neaten them. Sew the valance around the bed.

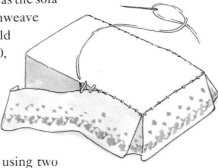

3 ▷ For the mattress, cut a piece of wadding the same size as the base, and a piece of white evenweave or other white material 21 x 14cm (8¼ x 5½in). Press a 5mm (¼in) seam allowance on all sides, and lay the wadding in the middle of the fabric, on the wrong side. Turn up the sides of the fabric beside the wadding, and stitch seams at the corners, trimming away the excess fabric. The mattress cover is now shaped like the lid of a box.

4 ◁ Lay the mattress, wadding side down, on the base of the bed, and sew it to the base, covering the raw edges of the valance with the seam allowances of the cover.

5 ▷ Make the bedhead by lacing the embroidery to the plastic canvas bedhead. Sew the bedhead and base together up the sides, then ladder stitch across the bed base, pushing the needle through a hole in the plastic canvas bedhead and bringing it back through the next hole. Cover the back of the bedhead with white Jobelan evenweave. Cut a piece to fit, adding a seam allowance on all sides. Stitch it to the back of the bedhead turning in the seam allowance.

Making the Quilt

Work the pattern for the quilt on the violet coloured Jobelan evenweave. Following the chart on page 98, begin at the centre, judged by eye, and work each stitch over two threads of the fabric. Work all the cross stitches first, using two strands of thread together, before working the back stitches using one strand of thread only.

Wash and dry the fabric if necessary, and lay it right side down on the same-sized piece of white Jobelan evenweave. Stitch the pieces together around three sides.

◁ Turn right side out. Fill with wadding, then turn in the raw edges, and slip stitch together.

Making the Pillow

The pillow is made in the same way as the quilt. Work the design on white Jobelan evenweave measuring 6 x 8cm (2 ⅜ x 3⅛in). Back it with plain fabric, stitching around three sides, and turn the pillow right side out. Stuff with wadding, turn in the raw edges and slip stitch them together.

To make the Dressing Table

Work the dressing table top and edge, and the mirror frame on the white Aida. Prepare the fabric, marking each of the areas to be stitched with basting stitches, and leaving a suitable margin around each piece. Position the pieces on the fabric as shown in the diagram below. Mark the position of the mirror on the frame, and iron interfacing into this space. Following the charts on page 98, begin stitching at the centre of each piece, judged by eye, and work the designs using one strand of thread throughout. Work each stitch over one square, and work all the cross stitches before the back stitches.

The dressing table skirt is worked on the white Jobelan evenweave. Prepare as for the bed valance and the sofa skirt, see step 2, page 99, folding the fabric in half, and pressing a fold along the length of the fabric. Following the chart on page 98, work the design for the skirt on the top layer of fabric only, and leave a gap at either end to neaten the side edges.

Wash and dry the pieces if necessary. Oversew the side and top edges of the skirt together, turn in the side edges and hem.

Using the templates provided on page 102, cut out the plastic canvas pieces. Cut one back, one tabletop, one front, one mirror frame, two sides and two corners, and for the table edge, one front edge, two side edges and two corner edges.

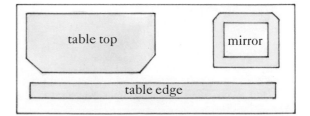

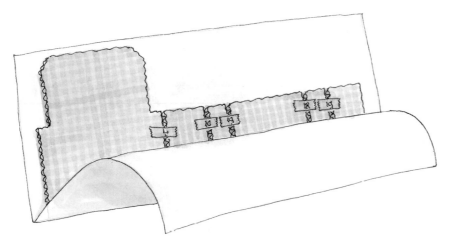

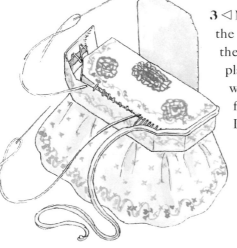

Assembling the Dressing Table

1 △ Make the inner frame by covering the pieces with sew-in interfacing. Lay them in a line as shown, beginning with the back. Hold the pieces together with sticky tape and sandwich them between two layers of interfacing, over-sewing the edges and trimming away the excess fabric. Join the seam between the side and back pieces.

2 ◁ Run a gathering thread along the top edge of the skirt, and pull it up until the skirt fits the front edge of the dressing table from one side to the other. Stitch the skirt to this edge.

3 ◁ Mount the table top on the plastic using the lacing or sandwich method and sew it to the top edge of the dressing table. Lay the plastic table edge pieces in a line on the wrong side of the embroidered edge as follows: side-corner-front-corner-side. Lace the fabric over the plastic and turn in the ends to neaten them. Sew the edge to the table, and cover this seam with white braid.

4 △ Mount the mirror frame on the plastic. Follow the instructions in the techniques section on page 109 to make the opening for the mirror. Stick the mirror card to the back and sew the frame in position around the outside edge. Stitch the bottom edge to the table, and cover the seam with braid. Stitch another length of braid to the sides and top of the mirror frame.

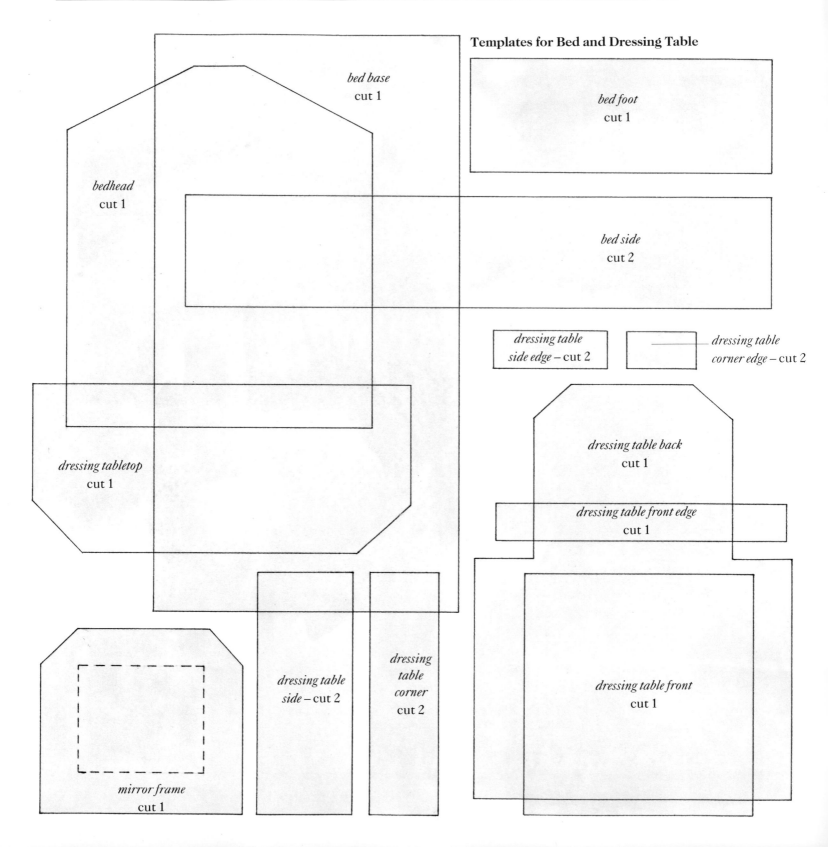

Templates for Bed and Dressing Table

bed base
cut 1

bed foot
cut 1

bedhead
cut 1

bed side
cut 2

dressing table side edge – cut 2

dressing table corner edge – cut 2

dressing tabletop
cut 1

dressing table back
cut 1

dressing table front edge
cut 1

dressing table side – cut 2

dressing table corner
cut 2

dressing table front
cut 1

mirror frame
cut 1

Cot for the Nursery

Nurseries can be amongst the most enchanting of doll's house rooms. This cot is made using blue fabric but it would be a simple matter to change the colour scheme.

Measurements
The finished size of the cot is 8cm tall, 5cm wide and 7.5cm long (3¼ x 2 x 3in), but the skirt may stick out and make it appear larger.

Materials
- *For the lower frill and quilt*: Piece of pale blue 28-count country-style evenweave measuring 62 x 10.5cm (24½ x 4⅛in)
- *For the top frill and inside of cot*: Piece of white 28-count Jobelan evenweave measuring 45 x 17cm (17¾ x 6¾in)
- Wadding measuring 7.5cm square (3in square)
- *For the inner frame*: Piece of white sew-in interfacing measuring 23.5 x 8.5cm (9¼ x 3⅜in)
- 1.5m (59in) of white lace, 1cm (⅜in) wide
- DMC or Anchor stranded embroidery cotton in the colours shown on the charts
- 7-mesh plastic canvas measuring 20.5 x 11.5cm (8⅛ x 4⅝in)
- Tapestry needle size 26
- Sewing needle
- Matching sewing thread
- Embroidery frame if required

To work the embroidery
Cut a piece of the blue country-style evenweave measuring 45cm x 8.5cm (17¾ x 3⅜in). Neaten the side and lower edges by oversewing and turn up a narrow hem along the lower edge 5mm (¼in) wide. Press this hem with an iron and stitch lace along it, placing the lace on the right side of the fabric, overlapping the bottom edge.

Starting at the right hand side of the fabric, embroider the design shown on the chart on page 105 for the lower frill. Each square represents two threads of the fabric. Work all the cross stitches over one square. Position the design three stitches up from the top edge of the lace, and use two strands of thread for the cross stitches, and one strand for the back stitches. Follow the chart for the position and colours of the back stitch. The pattern should be repeated five times across the width of the fabric.

Prepare the top frill from white Jobelan evenweave. Cut a piece of fabric 45cm x 4.5cm (17¾ x 3¾in). Oversew the sides and lower edge, turn up the lower edge and trim it with lace.

The head of the cot is embroidered on white Jobelan evenweave. Cut a piece 9cm x 8.5cm (3½ x 3⅜in) and mark the shape in the middle of the fabric, using basting stitches. Cross stitch the floral motif, using two strands of thread together.

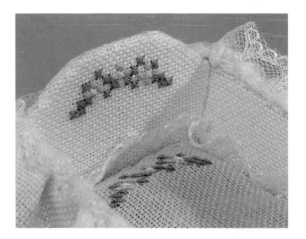

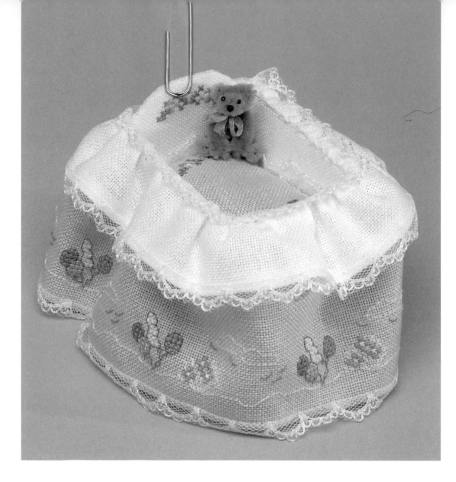

2 ▽ Make the inner frame of the cot by covering it with interfacing and stitching the side seam as described for the sofa in step 7 on page 94. Stitch the top of the cot to the base.

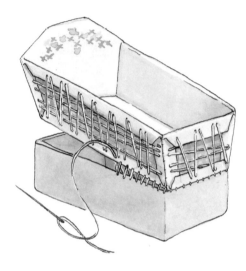

Wash and dry these pieces as described in the techniques section, on page 110.

Using the templates provided on page 105, cut the pieces for the cot from the plastic canvas. Cut one head, one foot, two sides and a bottom for the cot itself and two sides and two ends for the base.

To assemble the Cot

1 ◁ Cover the sides and foot of the cot with white Jobelan evenweave, using the lacing or sandwich method. Mount the embroidered head of the cot on the plastic canvas, and cover the back with white Jobelan. Cover the bottom of the cot with wadding before covering it with white fabric, as for the sofa seat, described in step 5, page 93. Stitch the sides to the head and foot, and stitch the bottom in position.

3 ▽ With right sides facing, stitch the sides of the blue lower frill together. Press the seam open so that it will lie flat, and turn the frill right side out. Gather around the top of the frill and pull it up until it fits around the top edge of the cot. Place the side seam at the corner between the cot head and the right hand side, and oversew the frill to the cot. Stitch the frill across the back of the head, not around the top edge.

4 Stitch a side seam in the white frill as for the blue frill, but turn the top edge over before running a gathering thread around it. Draw up the gathers and stitch the white frill to the top edge of the cot, covering the raw edge of the blue frill and placing the side seam at the top right hand corner. Cover the edge with lace.

Making the Cot Quilt

Make the quilt in the same way as for the bed, described on page 100. Cut two pieces of fabric from the blue evenweave, each measuring 8.5 x 10.5cm (3⅜ x 4¼in). Following the chart opposite, work the design onto one piece of fabric, and use the other to back it. With right sides facing, stitch around three sides. Turn right side out and stuff the quilt with wadding. Turn the raw edges inside and stitch them together. Sew lace around the outside edge of the quilt.

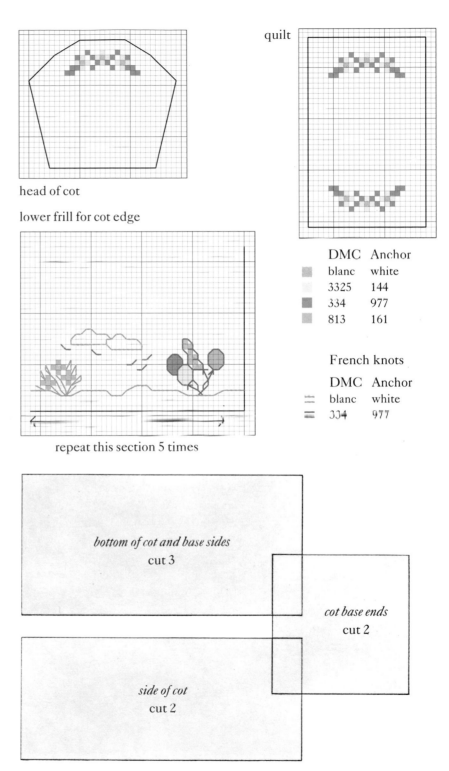

quilt

head of cot

lower frill for cot edge

repeat this section 5 times

	DMC	Anchor
	blanc	white
	3325	144
	334	977
	813	161

French knots

	DMC	Anchor
	blanc	white
	334	977

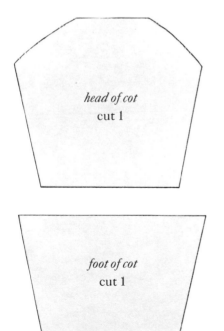

head of cot
cut 1

foot of cot
cut 1

bottom of cot and base sides
cut 3

cot base ends
cut 2

side of cot
cut 2

Toy Box for the Playroom

This colourful toy box could contain any number of delightful toys – trains, dolls or puzzles. Change the bright red colour to suit your own decor if you wish.

Measurements

The finished size of the toy box is 4cm tall, 6.3cm wide and 3.5cm deep (1⅝ x 2½ x 1⅜in).

Materials

- *For the sides and lid*: Piece of white 18-count Aida measuring 32.5 x 8cm (12⅞ x 3 ⅛in)
- *For the base and lining*: Piece of red felt measuring 18 x 11cm (7⅛ x 4⅜in)
- Piping cord, measuring 6.5cm (2⅝in)
- DMC or Anchor stranded embroidery cotton in the colours shown on the charts
- 7-mesh plastic canvas measuring 12.5 x 10cm (5 x 4in)
- Small button or bead (optional)
- Tapestry needle size 26
- Sewing needle
- Matching sewing thread
- Embroidery frame if required

To work the embroidery

Work the lid and sides on the white Aida. Prepare the fabric as described in the techniques section, outlining the areas to be stitched on the fabric with basting stitches. Make sure there is enough space between them as shown in the diagram below. Following the charts on page 107, begin in the centre, judged by eye, and work the design using one strand of thread only. Work each cross stitch over one square of the fabric, but some of the back stitches will be worked over more than one square, for example the letters A and V.

Wash and dry the fabric as described in the techniques section on page 110.

Using the templates provided on page 107, cut out the plastic canvas pieces. Cut one lid, one back, one front, two sides and a base.

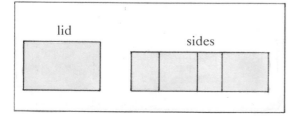

sides of
box

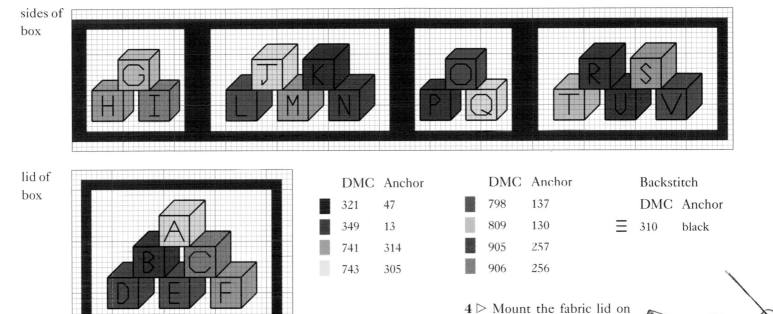

lid of
box

DMC	Anchor
■ 321	47
■ 349	13
■ 741	314
□ 743	305

DMC	Anchor
■ 798	137
□ 809	130
■ 905	257
■ 906	256

Backstitch

DMC	Anchor
≡ 310	black

Assembling the Toy Box

1 Separate the embroidered side piece from the lid and lay it face down on the working surface. Lay the plastic side pieces on the fabric, and hold them together with sticky tape. Lace the embroidered sides to the plastic pieces, making sure the corners are correctly positioned on the pattern. Ladder stitch the side edges together to make a box shape.

2 ◁ Cover the base with red felt and sew it to the sides of the box.

3 ◁ Cut a piece of red felt lining to fit inside the box sides, and stitch the ends together. Cut another piece to cover the base and sew it to the bottom edge of the felt sides, keeping the seam outside. Sew or stick the lining inside the toybox.

4 ▷ Mount the fabric lid on the plastic canvas lid. On the underside of the front edge sew the ends of the cord to the fabric 2cm (¾in) apart to make a handle. It should stick out beyond the edge of the lid.

5 Sew or stick red felt to the underside of the lid, covering the cord ends. Sew the back edge of the lid to the back edge of the box. If wished, sew the button or bead on the box front to fasten the cord.

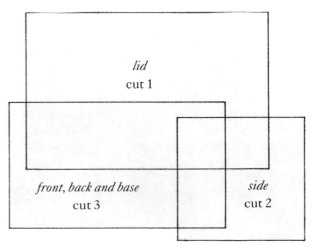

lid
cut 1

front, back and base
cut 3

side
cut 2

Materials and Techniques

This section gives further details on the materials used to make the three dimensional designs, and describes the techniques followed when stitching and assembling the pieces.

FABRICS AND OTHER MATERIALS

Aida and hardanger

These fabrics are used to make houses, boxes and vases. They are easy to stitch on because they are woven with distinct holes in a regular square pattern showing where to place the stitches. Each cross stitch is worked over one square of the fabric, and the number of squares per inch of fabric identifies the count. For example, hardanger has twenty-two holes per inch, and is referred to as twenty-two count. Aida comes in several different counts, ranging from twenty to eleven. The designs in this book are all worked on eighteen or twenty count Aida because of their miniature size.

Country style, Minster linen and Jobelan evenweaves

These fabrics are also woven with an equal number of threads in the width and length of a square of fabric, but they do not have distinct holes for your needle. They come in several different counts, but only twenty-eight count is used for these designs. Each stitch is worked over two threads giving fourteen stitches per inch of fabric. There is a wide range of colours, and the country style and linen types have some raised threads in their weave, giving a less smooth surface.

Felt

This is a useful non-woven fabric which will not fray when cut. It is not suitable for cross stitching but is used for some parts of the assembly process, and gives a neat finish to the underside of the pieces. It comes in a wide range of colours, and may also be found with self-adhesive backing.

Interfacing

Two types of interfacing are used in these designs: sew-in and iron-on. Make sure you use the type specified. Interfacing is another fabric that will not fray when cut because it is not woven. It is usually available in black or white and in a number of different weights. Choose medium weight for the sew-in interfacing needed for the sandwich method, and light or medium weight iron-on interfacing for making openings.

Plastic canvas

Plastic canvas is used throughout this book as a means of stiffening the pieces, not as a material for stitching. It is sold in sheets or as pre-formed plastic shapes. Make sure you buy a large enough sheet to complete the project you are working on. All these designs use 7-mesh plastic canvas, but it can be found in five, ten or fourteen mesh and with various degrees of stiffness. The larger pieces may benefit from the use of "ultra stiff" plastic canvas, which is slightly thicker and more rigid. Always use a type with square holes, which is easier to cut to shape. Keep a pair of scissors especially for cutting plastic canvas. Do not use embroidery or dressmaking scissors, as you will spoil the blades. When cutting the shapes from the plastic canvas, use the templates provided. You can draw the shapes on the plastic before cutting them out, or make patterns to cut around. Use the plastic lines to form straight edges, and trim any plastic sticking out. When cutting a curved or diagonal edge make it as smooth as possible to prevent the plastic sticking through the fabric when you assemble the piece.

Threads

Stranded embroidery cotton Stranded cotton comes in skeins, with each length made up of six strands. The working instructions tell you how many strands to use for each part of the embroidery, but generally speaking, the cross stitching worked on Aida and hardanger uses one strand at a time, while the cross stitching on the Jobelan and linen evenweaves uses two strands together. Most of the back stitch uses one strand at a time, but you may use two for greater definition. French knots and bullion knots are generally worked using two strands of thread for a crunchy effect. The designs in this book were worked using DMC stranded cotton, but equivalent colour numbers are given for the Anchor range.

Metallic threads Gold or silver metallic threads give added sparkle to a design. DMC metallic threads are divisible into three strands, and the instructions specify how many strands you need. Madeira metallic thread has only one strand, and you will need to cut two strands to work the embroidery.

BASIC EQUIPMENT

Needles and tweezers

Work the embroidery using a blunt-ended tapestry needle, size 26 or 28.

Use whichever type of sewing needle you are most comfortable with for the lacing or sandwich method and for sewing simple seams. When you are stitching roofs to walls, or working round a tight corner, you may find it useful to have a curved needle. Whichever you choose, a pair of tweezers will help you manipulate the needle.

Other pieces of basic equipment you may find useful include pins, glue and a product such as "Fray Check" to prevent the fabric fraying. If you use glue, choose one suitable for fabric that will not seep through and spoil your stitching.

Embroidery frames

Some stitchers always mount their work in a frame, while others feel more comfortable without one. Working without a frame may distort the fabric, especially if the design includes areas of half cross stitch. The smaller pieces in this book are not suitable for circular frames but can be mounted on wooden square or rectangular frames. These can be bought as a set of sides of different lengths which interlock to give the most appropriate size for your work.

TECHNIQUES

There are three stages to making a piece of three dimensional cross stitch. First the design is embroidered on the fabric. It is then mounted on pieces of plastic canvas which will form an inner frame and provide support. Finally these pieces are sewn together to form the desired shape. At each stage specific instructions must be followed to enable the piece to be completed without mishap.

Preparing the fabric for the embroidery

The cross stitching must be correctly positioned on the fabric, surrounded by margins of at least 2cm (¾in) of unworked fabric which are essential for mounting the embroidery on the plastic pieces. Refer to the chart for the overall shape of each piece of embroidery, not just where the cross stitches are placed, and tack this shape onto the fabric, making sure it has suitable margins on all sides as shown in the diagram above. If more than one piece is stitched on the fabric, as for The Bothy on page 36, you will need to space them about 4cm (1½in) apart.

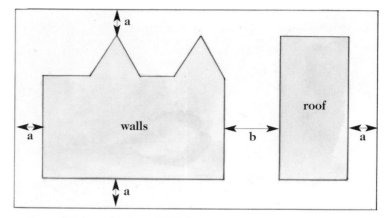

a: 2 cm (¾in)   b: 4 cm (1½in)

Work the embroidery within this shape. You will need the upper outline of the walls for the next stage. Begin stitching in the centre of each piece, but if the piece is an irregular shape, use your own judgement to start as centrally as possible.

When you are ready to mount the embroidery on the plastic you will need to separate any parts of the design that have been stitched on the same piece of fabric. Cut carefully between them, making sure that each piece has a wide enough margin around it on all sides.

Making an opening in the fabric

Some of the pieces have openings in the fabric, for example, the money boxes have slots and hatches.

1 ▽ Mark the position of the hole with tacking stitches and cut a piece of iron-on interfacing the same size as the hole. Iron it into the space before you begin stitching. If there is no embroidery, such as the base of the cartoon money box, mark the position for the hole using the plastic canvas shape as a guide and iron the interfacing into this space.

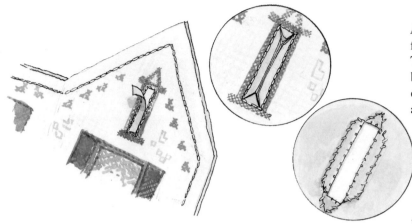

2 △ When you are ready to assemble the piece, first mount the fabric on the plastic canvas. If you are using the sandwich method, recommended for the money boxes, clock and jewellery box sides, back stitch around the edge of the hole once the plastic is sandwiched between the layers of fabric. Carefully cut the hole open, beginning at the centre and cutting diagonally into each corner. Do not cut the fabric away from the sides of the hole, but turn it inside. Turn your work over and slip stitch these pieces of fabric to the interfacing. Oversew around the hole to secure any stray threads, and use "Fray Check" to help keep the edges of the opening smooth.

◁ It is not necessary to use the sandwich method to mount the money box bases, the top of the vase or the dressing table mirror. For these pieces, cut open the hole as before, and lace it open. You will need to trim the fabric a little before lacing the mirror frame to the plastic canvas.

Making stays for openings
▷ The money boxes have stays around their slots and hatches. Each stay is made from a piece of plastic canvas covered in fabric so that it may be sewn around the opening. Use felt or interfacing. You can sandwich the stay between two layers of fabric by oversewing around the inside and outside edges.

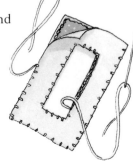

Alternatively, you can lace fabric to one side of the stay. This is a quicker method, but you may find it more difficult, as the stay is awkwardly shaped. ▷

Preparing the embroidery for assembly
When you have completed the embroidery, it may need to be washed before it can be mounted on the plastic, although it is better not to wash a piece embroidered with metallic thread. If you do need to wash the embroidery, use a mild cleaning agent suitable for hand washing. Use warm water and do not rub or scrub the stitching. Rinse the fabric well, and roll it up in a thick towel, do not spin or wring it dry.

Set your iron to a low heat, and fold the towel on the ironing surface, so that it is several layers thick. Place the embroidered fabric on the towel, right side down, and carefully iron the back, using a circular motion. The raised embroidery will be protected by the towelling and not flattened.

Leave the embroidery to dry thoroughly before you mount it on the plastic canvas frame.

For regular care of a three dimensional piece, dust with a dry cloth or pass the nozzle of your vacuum cleaner over it providing the suction is not too strong. If it is stained by accident, try washing the surface using warm water and a mild cleaning agent. Do not immerse the piece in water, but clean only the affected part, and use as little water as possible. Too much water may make the fabric sag. If necessary, remove the felt underneath the base and sew it back on afterwards. You may also use a suitable dry cleaning product, but first check that it will not damage the fabric.

STITCHES
Cross stitch is the principle stitch used to embroider these designs, so make sure you are confident working it before you embark on a project. Each of the designs has two or more charts showing where to place the cross stitches on the fabric. The charts are made up of coloured squares, each square representing one cross stitch, and the key shows which colour thread is used for each coloured square. Some parts of the design, such as the roofs for the scented houses, are worked entirely in back stitch so the chart shows only coloured lines.

Place the first cross stitch in the centre of a design. Sometimes the centre is marked on the charts but for irregular shapes, simply judge by eye. Follow the chart carefully and refer to it often. Don't worry if you make a mistake. Check to see if the design will be spoilt by your error. Using the wrong shade of green for a plant, or stitching brick markings in the wrong part of the wall are not important and you may not need to unpick your work.

Beginning to stitch

It is better not to tie a knot in the end of your thread when you begin stitching, as it will make a lump in the work. Pull the thread through the fabric, leaving a tail about 3cm (1¼in) long on the wrong side. Hold this in place and begin to work the cross stitches, catching the end of the thread in the stitches on the back of the fabric. When you come to the end of the piece of thread, pass the needle to the back of the work and run this end also through the underside of the stitching. With subsequent lengths of thread, run the needle through worked stitches on the back of your work to secure the end before you begin stitching. When you have completed all the stitches worked in one colour thread in one part of the design, fasten it off before moving to another area of the design.

Cross stitch Cross stitches are formed by two diagonal stitches, one on top of the other, slanting in opposite directions. Do make sure the upper stitches all lie in the same direction, otherwise the work looks messy and confused.

Bring the needle up at the bottom left corner of the square of fabric being worked. Make a diagonal stitch to the top right corner. Bring the needle up again at the bottom right corner and make another diagonal stitch to the top left corner. Many people prefer to work all the lower stitches of an area of cross stitch, then go back covering them with the top stitches. Work this way if preferred, or complete each stitch as you go.

Half cross stitch For this stitch, work the lower stroke of the cross only, not the top stroke. It is shown on the chart as a triangle covering half the square, with the colour usually sloping from the bottom left of the square to the top right. Half cross stitches are usually worked in groups to fill in windows or large areas of sky or grass with a pleasant misty effect.

Fractional stitches These are also shown on the chart as squares containing triangles, but not necessarily sloping from left to right. Where two fractional stitches are worked in the same square they are shown as two triangles of colour. These stitches help to define an irregular shape and give it a smoother outline, such as a face or the building bricks on the toy box. The chart for the clock contains both half cross stitches and fractional stitches, so follow the instructions to help you distinguish between them.

Back stitch This stitch is used to give greater definition to areas of cross stitch. Work any back stitching after the cross stitches, as some of the back stitches will lie over the cross stitches. Most back stitches are worked over one square of fabric, but sometimes they are worked over two or more squares, so follow the chart carefully when placing them.

Working from right to left, bring the needle up through a hole in the fabric, then take a stitch backwards to the next hole. Bring the needle up again two holes to the left and take another stitch one hole to the right. Back stitches can be horizontal, vertical or diagonal.

French knots These are useful to give a raised crunchy effect when stitching flowers or creepers against a wall.

Bring the needle up through the fabric, following the chart for the position of the French knot. Hold the thread taut, and wind it two or three times around the needle without letting it become loose. Push the needle back down the same hole, or close to it, keeping the thread taut, and allowing the thread wound around

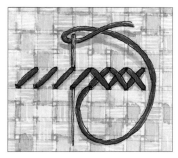
cross stitch

fractional stitch

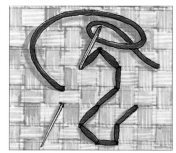
back stitch

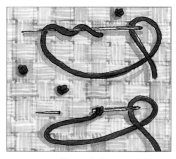
French knot

the needle to form a knot on top of the fabric. Many of the the French knots in these designs are positioned on holes in the fabric, but may be worked on the fabric weave if you wish. They can be made larger or smaller according to how many strands of thread you use, and how many times it is wound round the needle.

Bullion knots These knots form long sausage-shapes. Bring the needle up through a hole in the fabric. The knot will be formed between this point and the point where it re-enters the fabric, so take a small back stitch. Don't pull the needle through but bring it up again at the original point, keeping the needle in the fabric. Wind the thread five or six times around the needle, making sure the twists of thread are not too tight. Pull the needle through the fabric and the twists of thread, pulling away from the beginning of the stitch until the knot is lying flat on the fabric. Push the needle back down through the same hole as the end of the back stitch to hold the knot in place.

Ladder stitch This is a most useful stitch when assembling a three dimensional piece. It enables you to join two parts together with no thread on the right side of your work.

Attach the thread to one side of the work, and take a small vertical stitch along the fold on the other side. Return to the first side, take another small vertical stitch along this fold, and continue so that the stitches form "rungs" like a ladder. When you have made three or four rungs, pull gently on the thread, drawing the two edges together. If you are working around a difficult corner, leave the stitches loose until you have negotiated it, then pull the two edges together. The plastic canvas pieces may be pushed out of shape if necessary when you are stitching them together, but make sure they resume the correct shape afterwards.

bullion knot

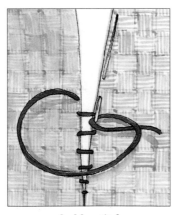

ladder stitch

Suppliers

Fabric
Fabric Flair Ltd
Unit 3
Northlands Industrial Estate
Copheap Lane
Warminster
Wiltshire
BA12 0BG
Tel: 01985 846400
(*Suppliers of all types of embroidery fabrics and a variety of accessories*)

Threads
DMC Creative World
Pullman Road
Wigston
Leicester
Leicestershire
E18 2DY
Tel: 0116 281 1040

Embroidery Frames
Siesta
P O Box 1759
Ringwood
Hampshire
BH24 3XN
Tel: 01425 473278

Plastic Canvas
Craft Depot
Somerton Business Park
Somerton
Somerset
TA11 6SB
Tel: 01458 274727
(*Suppliers of plastic canvas sheets and shapes and many other craft products*)

Clock Parts
A.G. Thomas (Bradford) Ltd
Tompian House
Heaton Road
Bradford
BD8 8RB
Tel: 01274 497171
(*Suppliers of clock movements and hands*)

Kunin Felt
Hantex Ltd
Unit 8-9, Lodge Farm Units
Wolverton Road
Castlethorpe
Milton Keynes
MK19 7ES
Tel: 01908 511428

Acknowledgements

For ideas, inspiration, support and friendship: Mike, Elizabeth, Annie, Keith and Janet Evershed, Jane Broadbent, Jennifer Davall, Tim O'Brien, Lindsey and Verena Walder, the Turner family and all their staff at Fabric Flair.